Frederick Good

General Automobile Workshop Manual

ines, Carburetors, Electrical Systems, Construction, Operation, Adjustment and Repair

(1922)

Frederick Good

General Automobile Workshop Manual

Engines, Carburetors, Electrical Systems, Construction, Operation, Adjustment and Repair (1922)

ISBN/EAN: 9783845711645
Erscheinungsjahr: 2011
Erscheinungsort: Bremen, Deutschland

www.unikum-verlag.de | office@unikum-verlag.de

Frederick Good

General Automobile Workshop Manual

ines, Carburetors, Electrical Systems, Construction, Operation, Adjustment and Repair

(1922)

PREFACE

THE purpose of this outline of experiments is to provide a progressive series of study-units in three groups which will serve as a basis for the organization of laboratory automobile classes for beginners. The course covers a systematic introduction to the automobile mechanisms and a study of their fundamental principles. It includes practical work, dealing with manipulations, disassembling and assembling of parts, testing for and locating troubles, making adjustments, and doing minor repair work.

The actual school conditions under which automobile classes must be conducted place certain unavoidable limitations upon the organization and the methods of laboratory work. We may assume that teachers must handle at least fifteen or twenty students in a class. It is also assumed that part of the time of the course will be devoted to discussion, demonstrations, and quiz work, using as a basis one of the automobile textbooks. In the teaching of large groups in automobile laboratory work teachers frequently resort to the squad method, in which the students are instructed and quizzed as a group around the apparatus. In the use of this method students are required to answer specific lists of questions or to write reports on the work.

In order to provide for the development of self-reliance, skill, and initiative, it is desirable in the automobile course, as in other laboratory courses, to plan for as much individual experimental work as the instructor is able to supervise efficiently. In the author's classes, students are permitted to work in groups of two, but not in larger groups. Many experiments require two people for the manipulation. Individual work is required in the setting up of illustrative apparatus, in operating mechanical and electrical units, and in disassembling or operating parts of the assembled chassis. Too much emphasis upon the lecture and demonstration methods results in developing a talking acquaintance with the automobile mechanism at the expense of manipulative skill.

In regard to equipment, the course as outlined herein requires a minimum of two automobiles,—the one a Ford chassis, the other the chassis of one other typical automobile. In the author's laboratory the large automobile is kept in running condition at all times and the engine is not used for disassembling. A flexible metal hose carries the exhaust gases from the muffler to the outside of the building. The front and rear axles of both laboratory automobiles are mounted on wooden stands, permitting the wheels to revolve. A 1½ horsepower gasoline engine mounted on a hand truck is used for preliminary engine study. The laboratory is provided with both gas and direct-current electricity. The gas engine and the automobile engine may be operated either by illuminating gas or by gasoline. The materials used in the experiments of this book should be regarded merely as a minimum equipment. If necessary, automobiles and many special parts may be purchased from a dealer in used cars and used parts. They should, of course, be fairly recent models. Used machines may be cleaned with kerosene or gasoline and painted. The cost of a minimum equipment for the course is between $1,000 and $2,000.

In the author's laboratory a cabinet of twenty compartments is used for storing special parts required as MATERIALS in the experiments. The compartments are numbered and labeled with the titles of the experiments for which they contain apparatus. An index is posted showing exactly where materials for any particular experiment may be found. Students are required to select their experiments *with the approval of the instructor* and they are required, at the beginning of the period, to give to the instructor a slip of paper containing their names, the date, and the title of the experiment upon which they intend to work. Students are held responsible for returning the apparatus to the proper cabinets when experiments are completed. A complete list of apparatus including cabinets with the names and addresses of dealers and manufacturers may be found on page 177.

Reference work has been included as a prominent part of the laboratory course. This provides for training in the use of the standard sources of information in connection with the manipulative and experimental exercises. A laboratory reference shelf is provided for the necessary reference books. See reference book list on page 175.

The author wishes to express to many teachers and students of Teachers College his appreciation for their suggestions and criticisms and for their cooperation in reading the manuscript, especially to the following professors: John F. Woodhull, Otis W. Caldwell, Frederick G. Bonser, Arthur D. Dean, and David Snedden.

The author is deeply indebted to John B. Bryan and to Edward Trauth, former students, who assisted in the organization and instruction in Automobile Mechanics at the time of the War Emergency Courses; to George D. Henck, Supervisor of Manual Arts, Pasadena, California; to Frank C. Panuska, Instructor in Mechanical Drawing, Stuyvesant High School, New York City; and to William H. Stewart, President of the Stewart Automobile School, New York City, for their careful reading of the manuscript.

Acknowledgment is hereby made to the Macmillan Company for the privilege of using certain line drawings and a part of the text from the author's book *Laboratory Projects in Physics*, to Professor James A. Moyer for permission to reproduce several illustrations from his *Gasoline Automobiles*, to the University of Wisconsin Extension Division for the use of several illustrations from Hobbs, Elliott and Consoliver's *The Gasoline Automobile*, and to the Van Nostrand Company for the use of illustrations in Frazer and Jones' *Motor Vehicles and Their Engines*.

F. F. Good.

New York, N. Y.
June, 1922.

DIRECTIONS FOR STUDENTS

The introductory experiments of Group I should be performed before taking up work in Groups II and III. Before beginning an experiment get the instructor's approval. Write the title of the experiment, your name, and the date on a slip of paper and give the slip to the instructor. This entitles you to the use of the apparatus necessary for the experiment. In general, students are permitted to work in pairs (not in larger groups).

The apparatus for some experiments is stored in cabinets. Consult the index showing where materials may be found. Many of these pieces of apparatus are expensive. Handle them with extreme care. After an experiment is approved by the instructor students are expected to take the apparatus from the cabinet to the tables, set it up and operate it according to the directions. If any of the required materials are not found in the proper cabinet, write on a slip of paper the names of the articles needed with your name and give it to the instructor. He will then give you the apparatus. When the experiment is finished return the special apparatus, personally, to the instructor and get your slip from him as a receipt for its return. Do not disassemble the apparatus until you are certain that you understand it fully. When an experiment is completed, students are required to disassemble the apparatus and place the parts in the proper cabinets. Your place at the laboratory tables should always be left in good order.

In doing mechanical work it is very important that students develop habits of careful and orderly procedure. Do not begin an operation until you understand with reasonable clearness what to do. In disassembling apparatus place parts in orderly arrangement. Do not use a hammer or other tool that may injure delicate parts of apparatus. Learn to use screw drivers and wrenches properly. If you are in doubt about any procedure, consult the instructor.

A carefully written record of each experiment that is performed should be kept in a loose-leaf notebook of uniform size. Write the title and the number of the experiment, your name and the date at the top of each report. Answer questions in complete sentences according to the numbering in the directions. Make clear diagrams of apparatus. They will help you to understand and remember the important facts of the experiment. Your laboratory report should show to the instructor at a glance whether or not you understood what you were doing. It should also aid you in reviewing the experiment for a test with a minimum expenditure of time.

Much of the value to be gained from this study of the automobile will depend upon whether you can improve your ability to take apart and put together mechanical units; to make them work properly; to understand how the different parts contribute to the proper functioning of the whole mechanism; to find out what is wrong if they do not work properly; to correct the trouble; and to learn the fundamental principles of their operation.

CONTENTS

AUTOMOBILE LABORATORY MANUAL

---

1. AUTOMOBILE MECHANISMS—A. SURVEY WORK

Identification of Important Parts and Their Functions

MATERIALS. Chassis of a typical automobile with rear wheels raised; textbook and reference books.

Examine the main divisions of the mechanism of an automobile chassis. In the textbook and reference books locate a number of line drawings or sectional illustrations showing the typical automobile mechanism with parts labeled. If possible, examine illustrations showing both horizontal views and vertical views. Proceed to the laboratory automobile and point out the parts shown in the illustration. The chassis may be divided into parts as follows: (*a*) the power plant, (*b*) the power-transmission system, (*c*) the control system, (*d*) front and rear axles, (*e*) the frame and springs.

1. State the make and the model of the car that you are studying.

2. Name in order of size twelve important divisions or parts of an automobile mechanism.

3. Beginning at the front of the car list the twelve divisions or parts, proceeding from the front toward the rear. When parts are grouped together name them in any order.

4. State in a sentence the function of each of these twelve parts in relation to the general operation of the car.

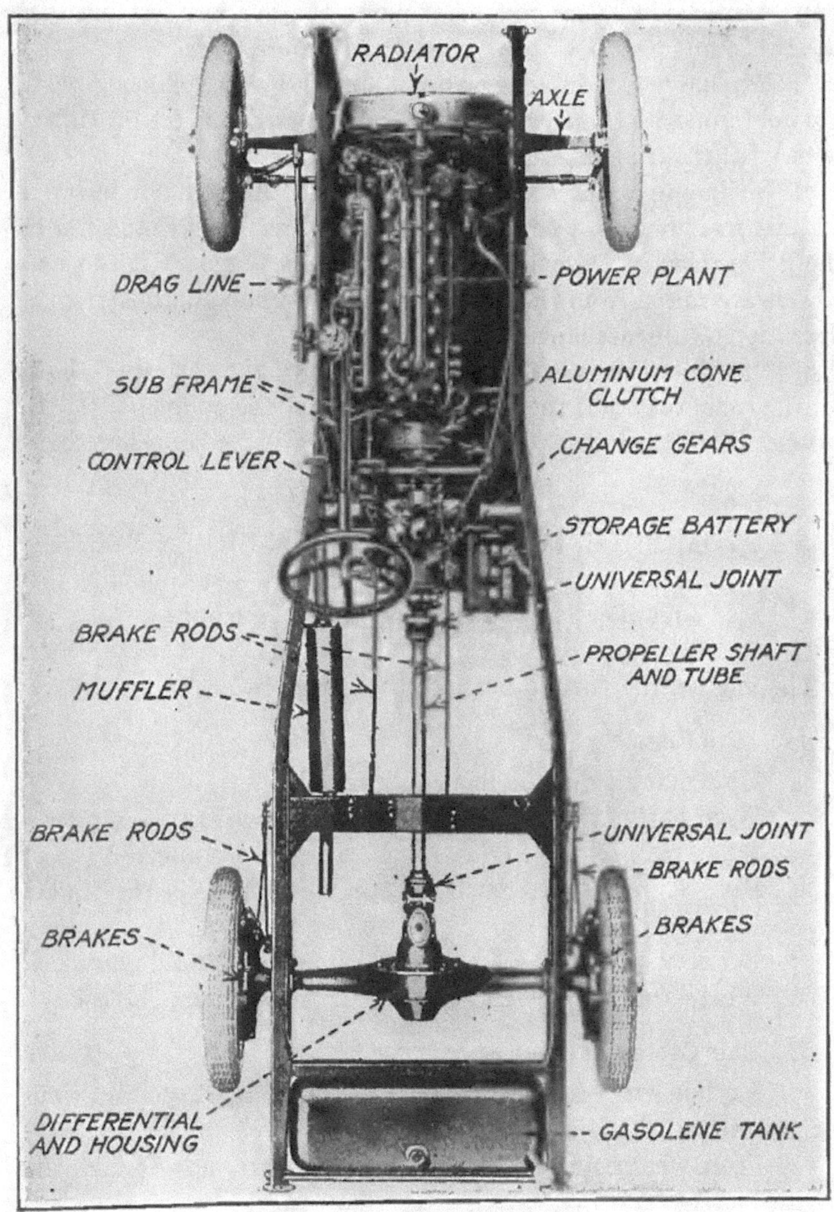

FIG. 2.—Plan view of a typical car.

5. According to your judgment name the five heaviest units of the car, omitting the wheels, axles, frame, and body.

6. Explain briefly in your own language how the following parts are held in position: (*a*) the engine, (*b*) the radiator, (*c*) the differential, (*d*) the change gears, (*e*) the carburetor.

7. Beginning at the starting handle at the front, name in order at least five important parts of the mechanism which connect with the drive-shaft between the crank and the rear axle. If the rear wheels are raised from the floor, crank the engine and observe the operation of the mechanism. Shift the gears.

8. Describe the location of the following: (*a*) crankshaft, (*b*) the carburetor, (*c*) the universal joint, (*d*) the cylinders, (*e*) the clutch, (*f*) the gearcase, (*g*) the crankcase, (*h*) the propeller shaft.

2. AUTOMOBILE MECHANISMS—B. SURVEY WORK

Identification of Parts and Their Functions

The engine, the cooling system, the carburetor.

A. **The Engine.**

1. How many cylinders has this engine?
2. What part of the engine moves up and down in the cylinder?
3. What part of the engine revolves in the crankcase?
4. Between what two parts of the mechanism is the intake manifold placed?
5. Between what two parts is the exhaust manifold placed?
6. Where are the inlet valves located? the exhaust valves?

B. **The Cooling System.**

7. Explain why engine cylinders are made with double walls for carrying a water-jacket.

8. From what point on the radiator does water flow toward the engine?

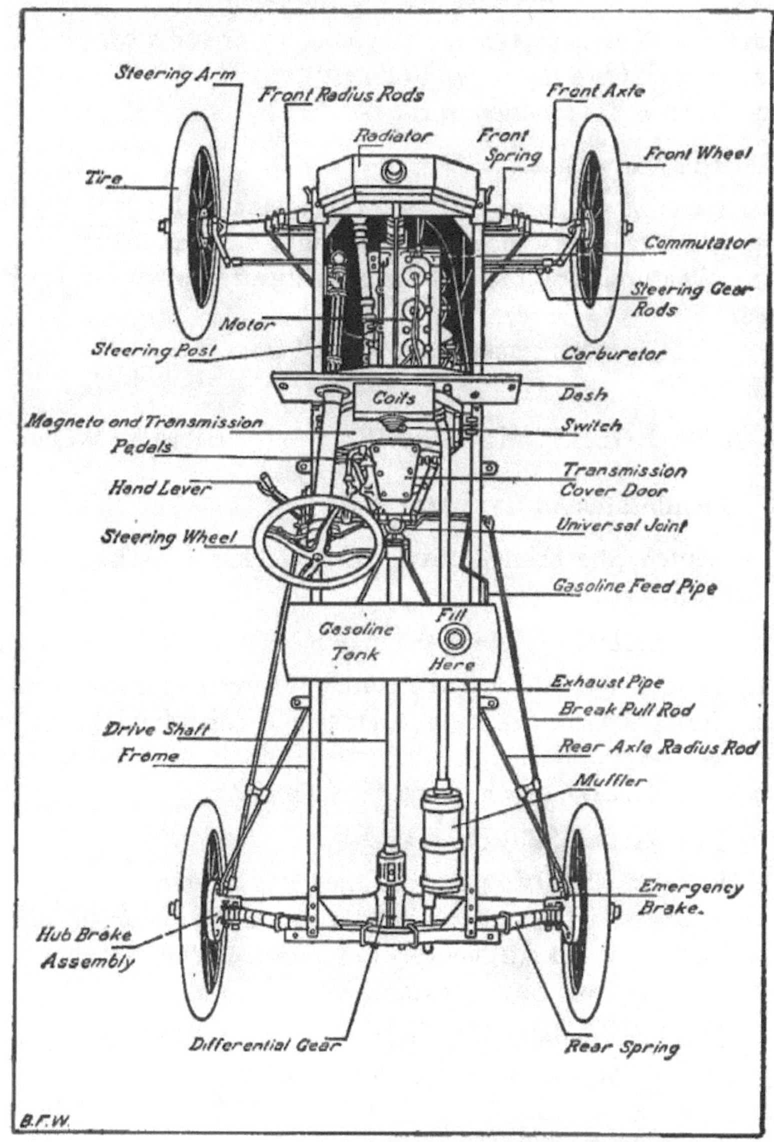

From Good's "Laboratory Projects in Physics." Used by permission of the Macmillan Company, publishers

FIG. 3.—The Ford car—Location of important parts.

9. How does the water return again to the radiator?
10. What causes the water to flow?
11. What is the function of the radiator?

C. **The Carburetor.**

12. Describe the location of the carburetor on this automobile.
13. What two substances are mixed in a carburetor?
14. What valve on the carburetor is operated from the steering wheel?
15. What valve is sometimes operated from the dash?

3. AUTOMOBILE MECHANISMS—C. SURVEY WORK

Identification of Important Parts and Their Functions

The clutch, the change gears, the differential, the brakes, and the control system.

A. **The Clutch.** Operate the clutch.

1. What two shafts does the clutch connect and disconnect?
2. State two situations in operating a car when the driver might use the clutch.
3. How does the driver operate the clutch?

B. **The Gears.** Shift the gears.

4. Between what two parts are the gears located?
5. Why is it important to have gears on an automobile?
6. How many speeds has this car? Name them.
7. What is meant by "gears in neutral"?

C. **The Differential.** If the rear wheels are raised, turn one and note the effect on the other. This mechanism may be studied in detail later.

8. Where is the differential located?
9. What trouble would arise in turning a corner if the rear axle were a solid rod from wheel to wheel?

D. **The Brakes.** Operate the brakes.

10. Where are the brake drums located?

11. What levers are used for applying friction to the brake drums?

12. How is the force applied at the levers transmitted to the brakes?

E. **The Control System.**

13. The steering wheel moves the steering knuckles and the tie bar. Locate (*a*) the steering knuckle and (*b*) the tie bar.

14. Get on the car and turn the steering wheel. What is the function of the tie bar?

4. THE GASOLINE ENGINE—A

Proportions of Mixture and Ignition

MATERIALS. Gas engine; ignition-bottle; large glass jar; rubber tube; induction coil; four dry cells; telephone magneto with small lamp.

A. **The Explosive Mixture.** Fill the ignition-bottle with water and invert in the glass jar of water. Attach the rubber tube to a gas cock. Collect a half bottle of gas by displacement over water. Remove the bottle, allowing air to enter, forming a mixture of half gas and half air. Hold your hand over the end of the bottle and invert a few times to mix the air and gas. Remove your hand and bring a lighted match to the mouth of the bottle. Does the mixture burn?

1. Does a bottle of pure illuminating gas burn more or less readily than half air and half gas?

2. Vary the proportions of the mixture and determine from the report of the explosion approximately what proportions by volume of air and gas give the most effective explosion. Which gives the better explosive mixture, one-fourth gas or one-fifth gas?

3. What is meant by the statements that the mixture in an engine is "too rich" or "too lean"?

B. **Ignition, the Magneto and the Induction Coil.** The explosion in gas engines is caused by a spark from a magneto (electric generator) or from an induction coil operated by dry cells. Operate a magneto generator, causing it to light a small lamp. (*Caution.*

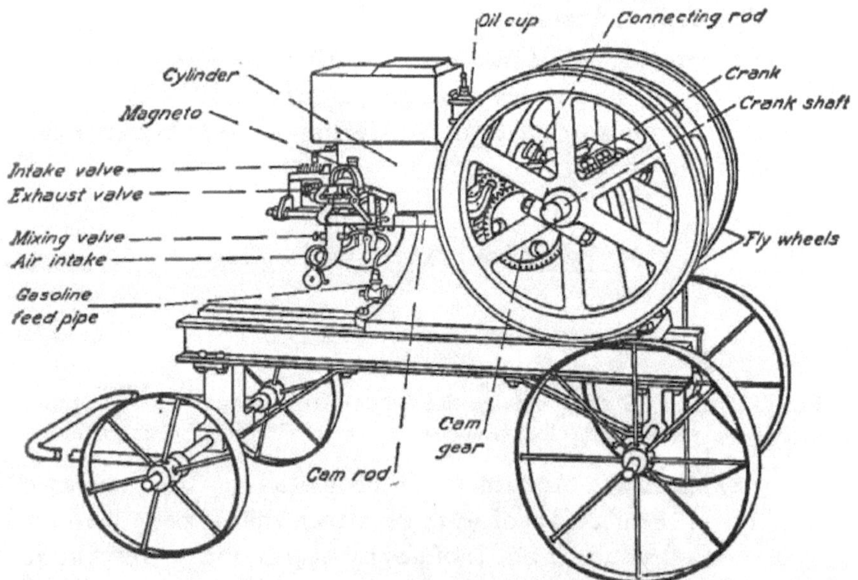

From Good's "Laboratory Projects in Physics." Used by permission of the Macmillan Company, publishers

FIG. 4.—A gas or gasoline engine.

An induction coil is dangerous. Do not touch the secondary terminals after attaching the battery to the primary.) Attach a wire from one secondary terminal of the coil to within a quarter inch of the other. This will form the spark gap. Connect one terminal of the battery of four dry cells to one terminal of the primary of the coil. Touch the other battery terminal to the primary terminal of the coil. The vibrator changes a continuous battery current to an intermittent current. An intermittent current in the primary causes a very high-voltage current to be induced in the secondary. This high-voltage current produces the spark for the ignition. (*Caution. To avoid the possibility of an accidental shock from the secondary terminals always disconnect the dry cells from an induction coil while working with the secondary circuit.*) Attach wires from the secondary terminals to a spark plug and operate it. Mount the spark plug in a ring-stand clamp.

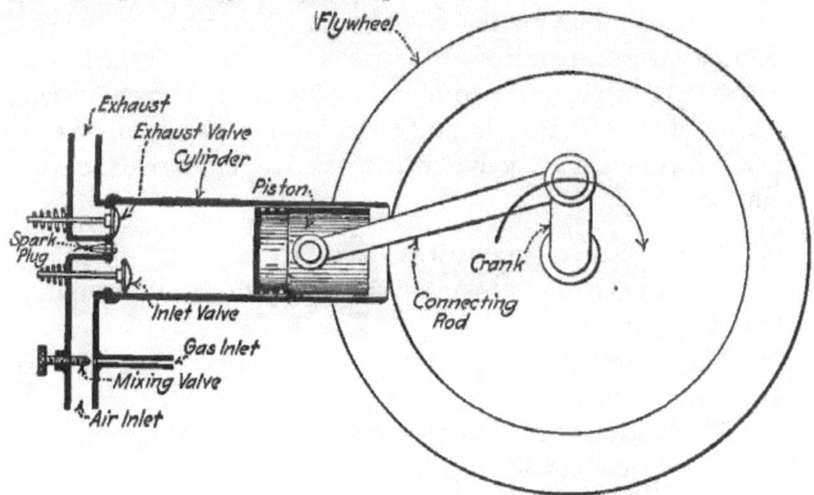

Fig. 5.—The principal parts of a four-stroke gas engine.

4. Diagram the wiring, showing induction coil, four dry cells, and spark plug with proper wiring. See Experiment 19.

A type of induction coil sometimes used in operating a gas engine is the simple "make-and-break" spark coil. It consists of a simple coil of many turns of wire with a soft iron core at the center This small type of coil gives a hot spark when the contact is broken. The igniter mechanism on the side of the cylinder operates the "make-and-break," furnishing a hot spark inside at the proper time. This is called a "make-and-break" system of ignition. When a spark plug is used as in an automobile it is known as a "jump-spark" system. The vibrator type of induction coil furnishes a jump spark.

The electric current for ignition may be produced by a magneto generator which is operated by the engine. As a source of ignition current the magneto is preferable to dry cells since dry cells will soon run down and require replacing.

C. **The Engine.** Before starting, fill the cylinder hopper with water. Oil the cylinder and bearings. This engine may be operated with illuminating gas instead of gasoline. The air and illuminating gas are mixed at the mixing valve. Ask the instructor to start the engine. Keep a safe distance from moving wheels. Observe its operation. Locate the following parts: mixing valve, cylinder, piston, inlet valve, exhaust valve, crankshaft, cam, and cam rod.

5. Make four diagrams representing the four strokes (half revolutions of a four-stroke engine). See *Practical Physics*, Millikan, Gale, and Pyle.

6. When the inlet opens what causes the explosive mixture to enter the cylinder?

7. What adjustment must be made at the mixing valve to get efficient working conditions?

5. THE GASOLINE ENGINE—B

Operation and Mechanisms

MATERIALS. One and one-half horsepower gasoline engine on a truck. See illustration of Gasoline Engine A.

A. **Starting the Engine.** Fill the cylinder hopper with water and oil the cylinder and bearings. Use illuminating gas or gasoline. Before attempting to start the engine throw on the spark-coil lever, close the choker (to increase the suction if gasoline is used), and turn the flywheels over compression. Open the air damper when the engine begins to fire. If the engine is properly timed, explosion should take place at or near maximum compression. If

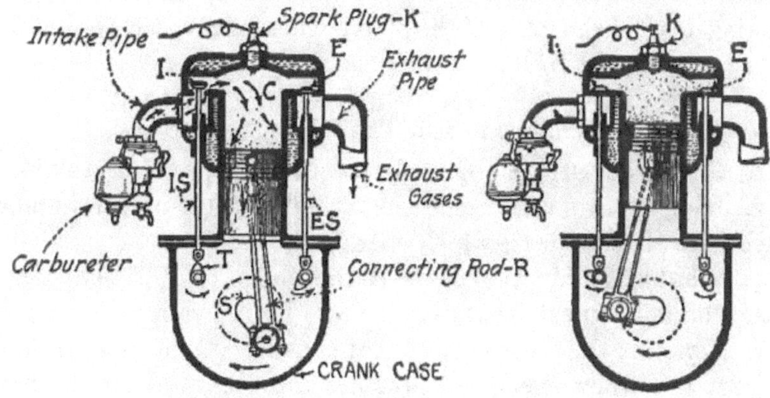

Intake position.

Compression position.

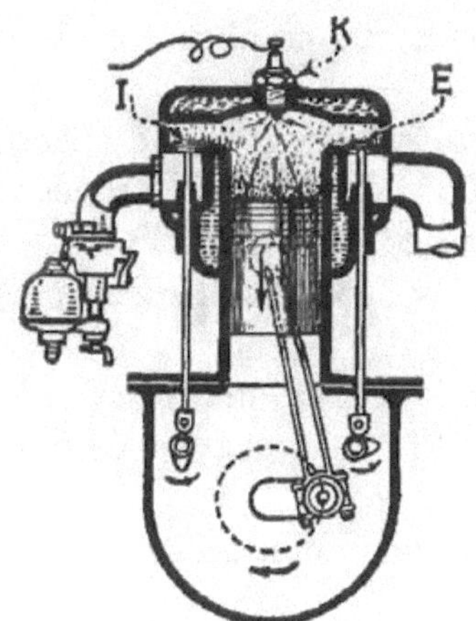

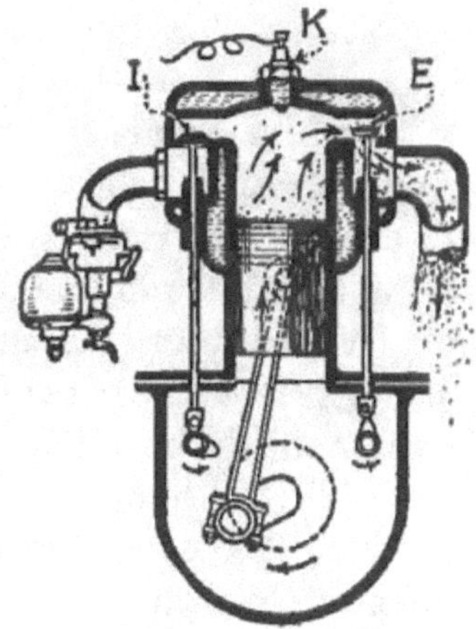

Explosion position.

Exhaust position.

Fig. 6.—The four strokes of an automobile engine.

you are in doubt about the procedure have an instructor start the engine. (*Caution. Keep a safe distance from moving wheels and shafts.*) The engine will start more readily if the mixing valve is opened about two turns to let in a richer mixture at the start. When the engine begins to run, the mixing valve should be screwed farther shut, otherwise the mixture may be too rich and cause smoking at the exhaust. If the mixture is too lean, the engine will misfire, run slowly, or "gasp for breath."

B. **Engine Mechanisms and Their Functions.**

1. Can a four-stroke engine fire every revolution? Explain.

2. In the four-stroke engine, what is the ratio of the number of teeth on the two gears which operate the cam?

3. What is the function of the cam?

4. Name two parts that are operated by the cam rod.

5. Examine the governor. What runs it? What does it do to the cam rod when the speed becomes too great? Pull the balls apart and note how this stops the firing when the engine is running. Set the speed lever in high, medium, and low.

6. What pushes the cam rod toward the crankshaft? What pushes it back?

7. When the engine is running, note that the cam rod operates a valve by means of a lever at the end of the cylinder. Is this the inlet valve or the exhaust valve? How do you know?

8. What is the purpose of the other valve? What causes it to open? What causes it to close?

9. What is the purpose of the water jacket around the cylinder? The water should be withdrawn from it in cold weather when the engine is idle. Why?

10. When the engine speeds up to maximum, what stops the sparking mechanism?

11. When the engine speeds up to maximum, what holds the exhaust valve open?

12. When the exhaust valve is kept open, does the piston draw in mixture through the inlet valve? Explain.

13. Why do gas engines need heavy flywheels?

14. After stopping the engine, throw out the switch at the spark

coil in order to avoid wasting the battery current. In what position would the make-and-break mechanism need to stand to exhaust the batteries?

6. CARBURETORS—A

The Principle and Construction of a Carburetor

MATERIALS. Bunsen burner; ignition-bottle; large glass jar; one or more sectional carburetors.

A. **Preliminary Work.** The purpose of a carburetor is to mix air and gasoline vapor in the proper proportion to obtain efficient combustion.

Note that a Bunsen burner has two adjustments—one for controlling the gas flow and one for controlling the air flow. The purpose of these adjustments is to mix air and gas in proper proportion before they reach the flame. A Bunsen burner is a carburetor.

1. Close the air inlet completely and light the burner. The flame is now operating with a " rich mixture "—insufficient supply of air. Describe the flame under these conditions.

2. Gradually open the air inlet of the burner until sufficient air is admitted to cause the flame to " strike back " to the bottom of the burner tube. This sometimes occurs in an automobile engine when the explosion " sneezes back " into the carburetor. Do not permit it to burn for more than a moment at the bottom. Describe the flame when the air inlet is open.

3. Fill the ignition-bottle with water and invert it in the jar of water. Allow illuminating gas from a rubber tube to bubble into the bottle, displacing the water. When the bottle is filled with gas, remove it and ignite the gas in the bottle with a match. In the same way remove the bottle when it is half full of gas, allowing air to mix with the gas so that you have a mixture of half

gas and half air. Try one-fourth gas and also one-fifth gas. Which burns most vigorously or forcefully?

B. **Carburetor Mechanism and Function.** Examine a carburetor in section. The common types of carburetors consist of two main compartments—the float chamber and the mixing chamber. The purpose of the float chamber is to hold a supply of gasoline from the tank ready for use in the mixing chamber. It must keep this supply at an approximately constant level. The purpose of the mixing chamber is to provide for mixing a fine spray of gasoline with the air as it is drawn through the carburetor by the suction of the engine. In answering questions refer to *Motor Vehicles*, Frazer and Jones (chapter on Elements of Carbure-

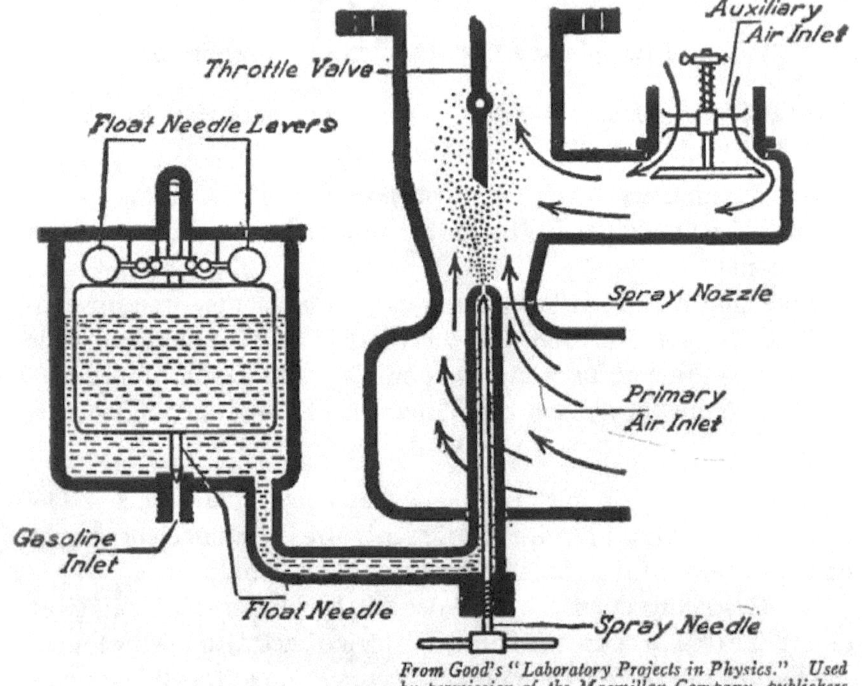

From Good's "Laboratory Projects in Physics." Used by permission of the Macmillan Company, publishers

FIG. 7.—A carbureter showing spray needle and auxiliary air inlet.

tion); *Gasoline Automobiles*, Moyer, or *The Gasoline Automobile*, Hobbs, Elliott and Consoliver.

4. What is the purpose of the float?

5. What is the function of the float needle?

6. Of what material is the float made?

7. Explain the sequence of operations which cause gasoline to enter from the tank into the float chamber (gravity system).

8. What causes gasoline to stop flowing from the tank?

9. What might cause a carburetor to flood (overflow)?

10. What is the function of a spray needle?

11. If the spray needle is too far closed, how is the mixture affected and vice versa?

12. Where is the choker or choke valve located, and what is its function?

13. How is it possible to obtain a richer mixture by means of the choker?

14. What is the function of the throttle?

15. Why does the mixture tend to become very lean when the throttle is nearly shut?

16. For what purpose is wire gauze used at the entrance to the float needle valve?

17. What is the purpose of the drain cock at the bottom of the carburetor?

18. What is a Venturi tube? See *Motor Vehicles*, Frazer and Jones.

7. CARBURETORS—B

Construction, Operation, and Adjustments

MATERIALS. A number of different makes of carburetors representing types with eccentric and with concentric float chambers. If possible, have one or more carburetors in section. Used carburetors are satisfactory.

A. **Carburetion.** When automobiles were first introduced, high-grade gasoline (volatile gasoline) was very cheap. Because the gasoline vaporized readily, carburetors were made in very elementary form—surface carburetors. As the demand for fuel increased, and with it the necessity for including in the fuel some of the heavier distillates, the problem of carburetor design and construction became more complex. Besides changes in the nature of the fuel, the demand arose for carburetors which would provide a more efficient mixture for wider variations in engine speed.

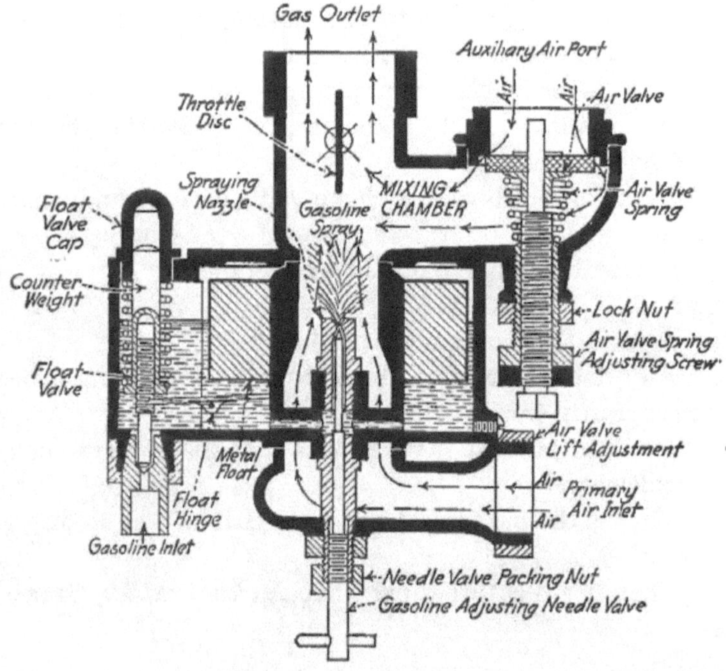

FIG. 8.—A carbureter with auxiliary air port and with concentric float chamber.

All simple forms of carburetors produce rich mixtures at high speed. If the mixing valve is set for high speed, the mixture is too lean for low speed. A simple carburetor that will produce a well-balanced mixture for all speeds has not yet been devised. Properly proportioned mixtures for the different speeds can be obtained approximately with complicated carburetors containing properly designed and adjusted auxiliary air valves. These carburetors are accordingly more expensive.

B. **Reference Work.** Use *Motor Vehicles*, *Gasoline Automobiles*, and *The Gasoline Automobile.*

1. What general type of carburetor is most commonly used at the present time?

2. Approximately what proportions by weight of air and gasoline give the best combustible mixture?

3. What proportions by weight give (*a*) the upper limit of combustion? (*b*) the lower limit of combustion?

4. Name four valves that may be found on many carburetors.

5. How does opening the throttle cause more air and gasoline mixture to flow?

6. Diagram a carburetor containing an auxiliary air port.

7. How does a metering pin differ from the ordinary spray needle?

8. What is meant by "concentric float chamber" and by "eccentric float chamber"?

9. State an advantage of the concentric type.

10. Should the float chamber of a carburetor be closed tight or should it have an opening in the top to let in air? Explain.

11. Why is the spray nozzle usually placed in a Venturi tube?

C. **Carburetor Adjustment.**

12. What is meant by "adjusting a carburetor"?

13. Name two valves common to many carburetors which usually require adjustment.

14. State six conditions that are necessary before making adjustments. See *Motor Vehicles.*

For a study of carburetor adjustments see experiments, Carburetors C, D, E, and F.

8. AUTOMOBILE ENGINE—A

The Construction and Operation of the Ford Engine

MATERIALS. Ford chassis, (used car—radiator, cylinder head, and one piston removed); reference books, *The Model T Ford Car*, Pagé, and *The Ford Manual.*

The most expensive and largest single unit of the automobile mechanism is the engine. Upon its design, material, and workmanship the efficiency of operation depends. An engine that is defective in design or adjustment may be very wasteful of gasoline. If the parts of the engine include cheap material and cheap workmanship, its life may be only half as long as it should be. The modern gasoline engine has required years of experimentation and the labors of many expert engineers. To appreciate it properly, an automobile driver should thoroughly understand its mechanical parts and the principles of their operation. The Ford engine has become famous because it is powerful for its size, it is efficient in the use of gasoline, and it stands up well under hard service.

A. **Mechanism and Operation.** This is an L-type motor. (Inlet and exhaust valves are on the same side. The T-type engine has intake on one side and exhaust on the opposite side.) In answering questions refer to *Ford Manual* and to *The Model T Ford Car*, Pagé.

1. Are these cylinders cast as a single unit (block) or in parts?
2. How many shafts are inclosed in the crankcase? Name them. What are their purposes?
3. How are the inlet and exahaust valves operated?
4. What operates the camshaft?
5. How many cams are on the camshaft?
6. How fast does the camshaft revolve with respect to the rate of the crankshaft?

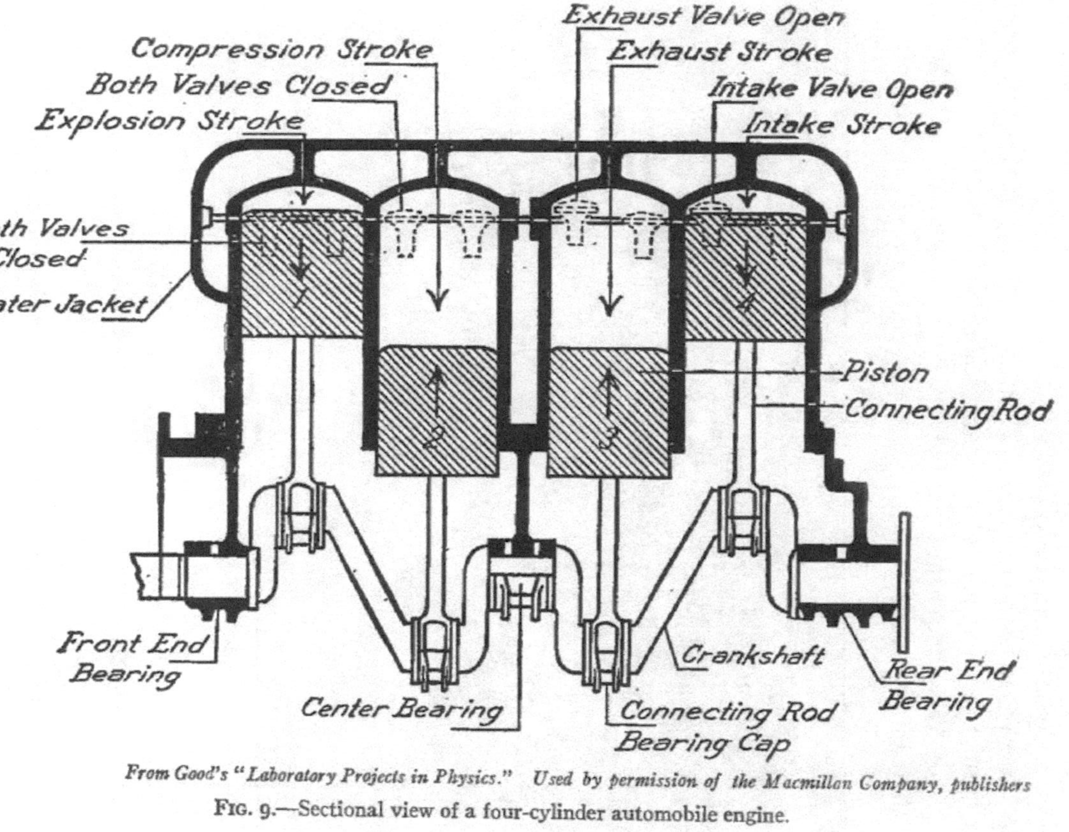

From Good's "Laboratory Projects in Physics." Used by permission of the Macmillan Company, publishers

FIG. 9.—Sectional view of a four-cylinder automobile engine.

7. What pushes the valves open?

8. What closes the valves?

9. What is the direction of motion of any piston, (*a*) when its inlet valve opens, (*b*) when its exhaust valve opens?

10. What important part of the ignition system is attached to the cylinder head?

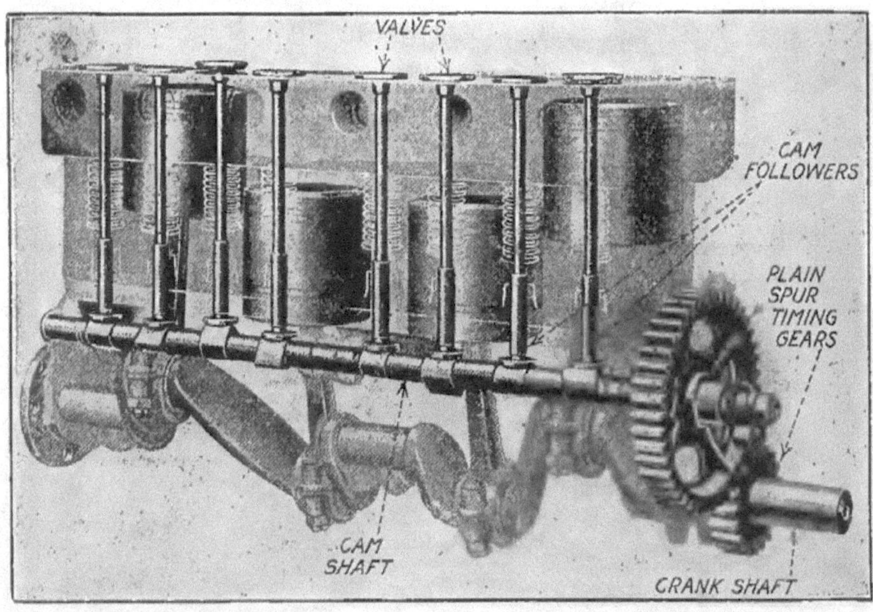

Fig. 10.—Phantom view of the Ford engine, showing timing gears, camshaft and mechanism.

B. **The Crankshaft.** Look into the open cylinder and observe the crankshaft. Have some one crank the car and you will note that the crankshaft revolves.

11. How many main bearings has the Ford crankshaft?

12. At what angle do the cranks stand with respect to each other in a four-cylinder engine?

13. How is the power transmitted from the combustion chamber to the crankshaft?

14. How are the crank bearings and the pistons oiled?

15. Name four important parts of the mechanism between the crankshaft and the rear wheels.

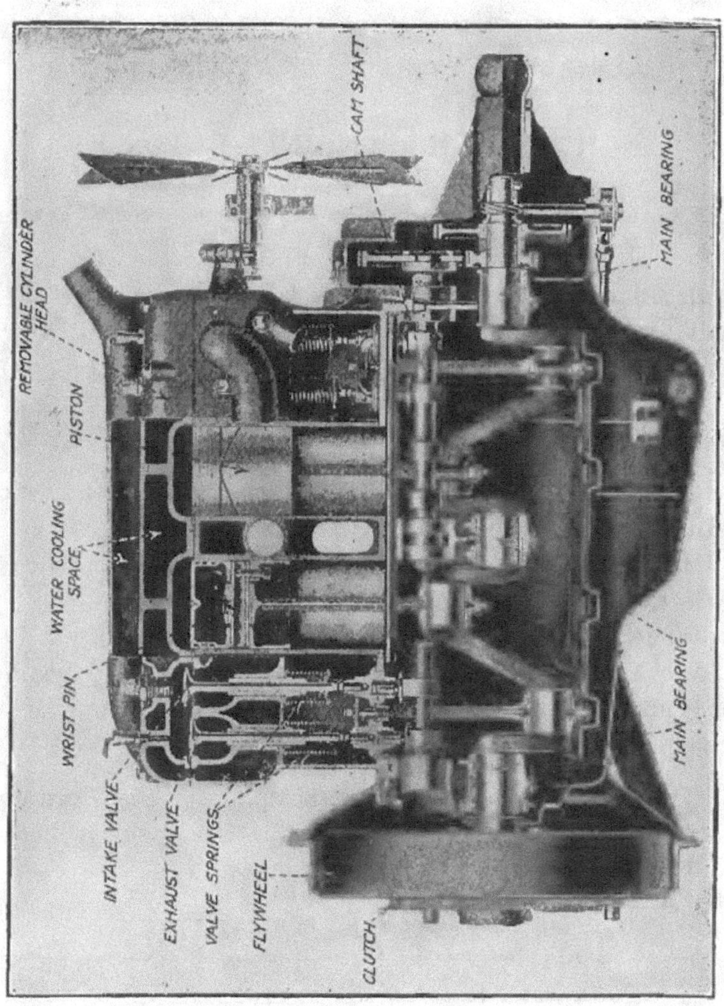

FIG. 11.—Sectional view of a typical four-cylinder engine.

C. **The Pistons.** One of the pistons has been removed for inspection. The connecting rod connects the piston to the crank-shaft.

16. How does a well-oiled piston aid compression?

17. How many rings has the Ford piston?

18. What is the purpose of the piston rings?

19. What kind of combustible mixture tends to deposit carbon on the piston and valves?

20. What causes old pistons to leak and lose compression?

9. AUTOMOBILE ENGINE—B. FORD

MATERIALS. Same as in Ford Engine—A. Reference book, *The Model T Ford Car*, Pagé.

A. **Ignition.** Remove the timer cap. The purpose of the timer is to regulate the time at which current is sent to each induction coil and consequently to each spark plug.

1. To which shaft is the timer attached?

2. How many contact points does the timer have?

3. What touches these points, sending currents to the induction coils and spark plugs?

4. How many sparks are produced in this four-cylinder engine for each revolution of the crankshaft?

5. Where is the magneto generator located in the Ford?

6. What is the sequence of firing in the cylinders, beginning at the front as No. 1? (Same as the sequence of opening of inlet valves.)

B. **The Cooling System.** (Thermo-siphon.) The Ford cylinders are cooled by convection. Examine the openings between the walls of the cylinder for water circulation.

7. Why is it necessary to have a cooling system?

8. What would be some of the results if the engine were operated without water in the cooling system?

9. In which direction does the water flow?

10. Explain what causes the water to circulate.

11. State two possible causes of trouble in the cooling circuit.

12. Name two chemicals that are commonly used to prevent freezing in winter?

C. **Lubrication.** The life of an automobile engine depends upon proper lubrication of the working parts. Automobile engine

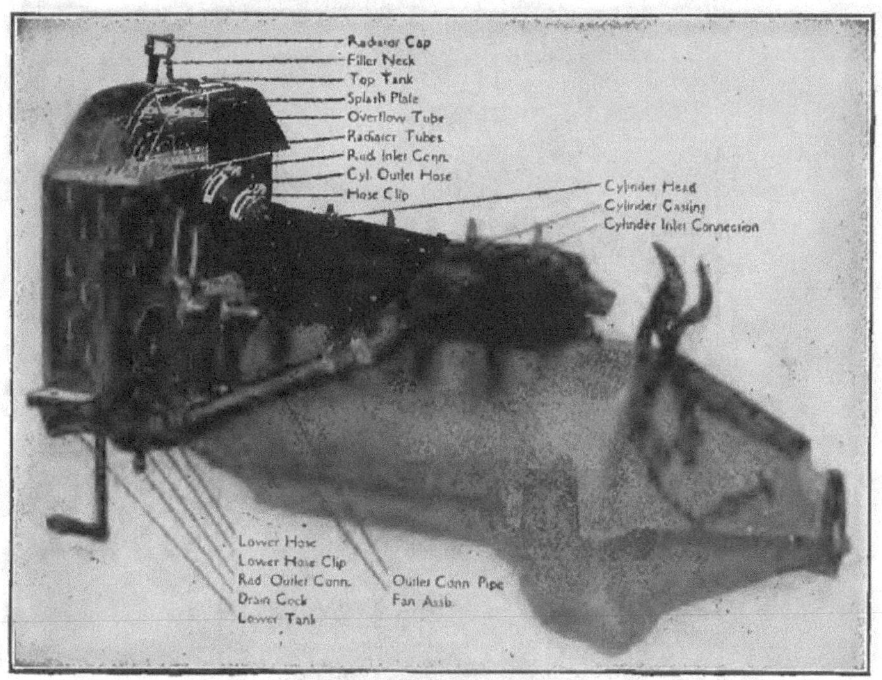

FIG. 12.—Ford cooling system.

pistons move at rates as high as one thousand to fifteen hundred feet per minute. The metal of the pistons, piston rings, and the cylinder wall will rapidly wear away unless a proper supply of oil is provided.

13. Explain the operation of a splash system of oiling.

14. What provision has the Ford for circulating the oil?

15. In what part of the crankcase does the oil stand?

16. If the engine should become overheated, what would be the effect upon the engine oil?

Fig. 13.—Full splash lubricating system on Ford car.

17. What parts of a crankshaft need oil?
18. What parts of a piston connecting rod need oil?

D. **The Manifolds.** Note the position of the intake manifold which carries the combustible mixture from the carburetor to the inlet valves. The exhaust manifold carries the burnt gases from the exhaust valves toward the muffler.

10. ENGINE-COOLING SYSTEMS—A

Air-cooling and the Thermo-siphon System

The firing of the mixture in a gas engine produces a temperature of between 2,000° and 3,000° F. The engine must be provided with some form of cooling system to prevent it from becoming overheated. Excessive temperatures would result in carbonizing and burning of the lubricating oil, warping of the metal parts, the rapid wearing away of the pistons and cylinders, and expansion of the mixture with the consequent loss of power. Strange as it may seem, more power is lost in an automobile in heating the cooling system than is utilized in driving the car. About one-fourth of the energy of the combustion is expended in driving the car. The rest is lost mainly through the exhaust and in heating the cooling system.

A. **Air-cooled Engines.**

1. Upon what conditions does cooling in the case of air-cooled engines depend? See *The Gasoline Automobile* or *Motor Vehicles*.
2. How is greater surface for air cooling obtained in the construction of motor cycle and other air-cooled engine cylinders?
3. Are large or small engines more suitable for air cooling? Why?
4. State two common objections to air-cooled engines.

B. **The Thermo-siphon Cooling System.**

5. For efficient operation, approximately what is the proper

temperature of the water surrounding the engine cylinder? See *Motor Vehicles.*

6. How does a thermo-siphon system differ from a pump system?

7. Does the water in a thermo-siphon system flow upward through the engine or downward? Why?

8. Beginning at the cylinder head, name all parts of the Ford thermo-siphon system which the water touches in making a complete circuit. See *Ford Manual.*

9. Examine the Ford engine with cylinder head removed. How many openings carry water from the water jacket of the cylinder casting to the cylinder head?

10. In the Ford how is the outlet from the cylinder head attached to the radiator?

11. How is the cylinder inlet connected to the outlet from the radiator?

12. Measure the approximate thickness of the water space around the Ford cylinder. Measure the approximate thickness of the cylinder wall.

13. Where is the drain cock on the Ford cooling system located and what is its function?

14. State two advantages of a thermo-siphon cooling system and two objections to it. See *Motor Vehicles.*

15. Name two types of radiator construction and briefly explain each. See *The Gasoline Automobile* or *Motor Vehicles.*

11. ENGINE-OILING SYSTEMS—A

Removing the Oil from the Engine and Refilling

MATERIALS. Two pails; a quart measure; strainer-funnel.

The lubricating oil of a gas engine is gradually decomposed by the heat generated in the cylinders. In order to keep the level of the oil in the crankcase at the proper height, it is necessary to add new oil as the old is used up. One of the products of decomposition of the oil is carbon. This deposits in the bottom of the crankcase. At regular intervals it is necessary to clean out this black residue which sometimes contains small particles of metal. Read in *Motor Vehicles* the part of the chapter on Lubrication dealing with draining and cleaning the crankcase. Place a galvanized pail under the engine of an automobile in such position that it is directly beneath the drain plug in the bottom of the oil reservoir. Remove the plug and drain the oil into the pail.

1. Is all of the oil removed in this way? Is all of the sediment removed?

2. Describe the usual method of removing the latter. See *Motor Vehicles*. How frequently should the cylinder oil be removed and the crankcase cleaned?

NOTE: Since this engine has not been operated sufficiently to necessitate the " flushing " of the oiling system with kerosene, this step may be omitted. Replace the plug in the crankcase. Do not omit the plug gasket or washer. Screw the plug tight enough to prevent leakage. Have this job inspected by the instructor before proceeding further.

3. What is the purpose of a plug gasket? Strain the oil, using the second pail, a small measure and strainer-funnel, and pour the strained oil into the engine through the filling tube provided for that purpose.

4. Keep a record of the number of quarts put in. How many quarts of oil should this engine have? See *Instruction Book*. Special care must be exercised to avoid spilling the oil on the car and on the floor. Place the pail under the drain plug as a precaution in case of leakage. Have this job inspected by the instructor after the oil is put into the engine.

5. How can you tell when enough oil has been put in?

6. What means is provided on a Ford engine for determining the proper level of oil in the crankcase? See *Model T Ford Car.*

7. Would an excess of oil do any harm? See *Motor Vehicles.*

8. What might happen if the oil level were allowed to get too low?

9. How does an excessive amount of lubricating oil manifest itself? See *The Gasoline Automobile* under Lubricating Troubles.

10. Describe fully how you would clean and replenish the oiling system of the Ford. See *Model T Ford Car.*

11. How often should the oiling system of the Ford be "flushed out"?

12. What kind of oil should be used in an automobile engine? See *The Gasoline Automobile* or *Motor Vehicles.*

13. What is meant by the following terms relating to lubricating oils: (*a*) flash point; (*b*) fire point; (*c*) cold point?

12. BRAKE MECHANISMS AND ADJUSTMENTS—A

Removing the Ford Rear Wheel and Study of the Brake Mechanism

Brakes employed for retarding or stopping the car are usually attached to the rear wheels. A cylindrical metal part called the brake drum is attached to the wheel. Against this drum a steel band may be drawn or released by force applied at the brake pedal or brake lever. The brake very commonly contains two bands, one which compresses against the outside and one which expands against the inside. There are, therefore, two general classes of brakes—external contracting and internal expanding. Read textbook on brakes.

A. **Removing the Rear Wheel of the Ford Car.** With a wrench take off the hub cap and the retention or clamping nut from one of the rear wheels of the Ford. Remove the wheel from the hub. Lay all parts aside in good order for reassembling. Have this work approved by the instructor.

1. What is the reason for using a cotter pin in the retention nut?

2. What is the purpose of the key which stands in the hub and axle grooves? In replacing the wheel do not omit the key.

3. If the key were not in place would it be possible to brake the car? Explain.

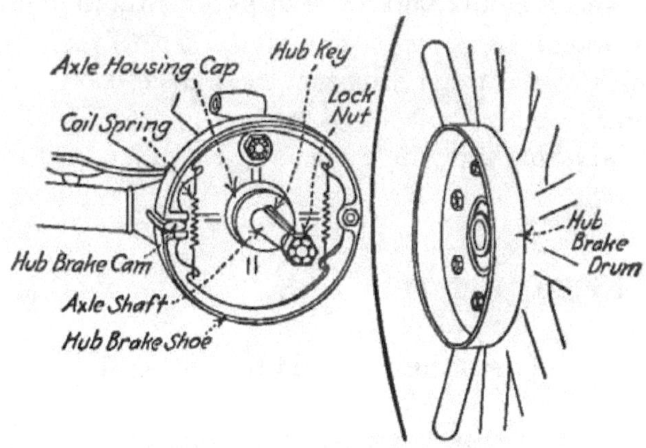

Fig. 14.—Ford emergency brake.

4. If the key were not in place would it be possible to drive the car? Explain.

B. **The Brake Mechanism.**

5. To which of the two general types of brakes does the Ford rear-wheel brake belong?

6. Diagram one type of external contracting mechanism and one type of internal expansion mechanism. See *Experiment 44*.

7. With a wrench remove the brake shoe. Have this work approved, then replace it. Name at least five important parts of the brake mechanism.

8. What causes the brake shoe to expand against the drum and what causes it to release?

9. Observe the hand-brake lever which operates the emergency-brake mechanism. By what means is the force carried from the brake lever to the expander shaft? See *Model T Ford Car.*

10. If the brake shoe becomes worn and does not engage tightly against the drum, what adjustments may be made to cause it to engage properly?

11. Note that the foot brake on the Ford tightens a brake band on the transmission mechanism. Is this a contraction brake or an expansion brake?

12. Which of the three drums on the transmission is the service brake drum?

13. Explain how applying the emergency brake also throws out the clutch.

13. INTRODUCTORY ELECTRICAL WORK—A

The Liquid Cell and the Dry Cell

MATERIALS. Base block $5 \times 5 \times 2$ ins.; round battery-jar $5\frac{1}{2}$ ins. high by $2\frac{3}{4}$ ins. in diameter; ammonium chloride (sal ammoniac); zinc battery rod; carbon rod from an old dry cell; Bunsen burner; electric bell; No. 24 insulated wire; jar of 10 per cent nitric acid, to be used only by the instructor; cardboard, for separating battery rods at top; short glass tube, for separating battery rods at bottom; glass stirring rod.

A. **Making a Leclanché Liquid Cell.** Make up an ammonium-chloride solution by filling the battery jar one-fifth full of ammonium-chloride salt and adding water till the top of the liquid stands 1 inch from the top of the jar. Dissolve by stirring with a glass rod. Place the zinc rod in the solution at one side of the jar, and the carbon rod at the other. Use a short piece of glass tubing at the bottom of the jar and carboard at the top to keep the electrodes separated. See instructor's model.

1. Connect wires to the electrodes and ring an electric bell.

2. Make a drawing of the cell indicating the materials used, and showing the direction in which the current flows. The current is considered as flowing from the positive to the negative electrode outside the solution. The negative electrode is the one acted upon more by the electrolyte. In this case the zinc is negative.

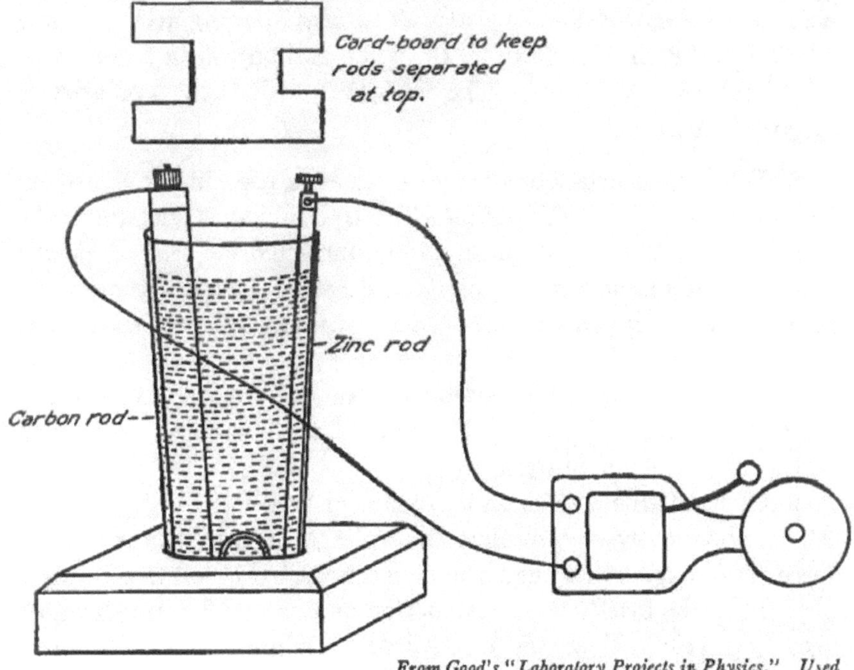

From Good's "Laboratory Projects in Physics." Used by permission of the Macmillan Company, publishers

Fig. 15.—A liquid cell—ammonium chloride.

B. **Polarization.** When this cell is attached to the electric bell it rings the bell for a short time and gradually becomes exhausted. This phenomenon is due to polarization. Hydrogen molecules are set free as a result of the chemical action. The carbon electrode gradually becomes covered with a thin film of hydrogen, which prevents the flow of the current. Polarization may be counteracted by placing in contact with the carbon electrode some form of oxidizing agent, as, for example, manganese dioxide. The hydrogen reacts with the manganese dioxide, forming water. This cell may be temporarily depolarized by heating the carbon rod in a gas flame for three minutes. It may be depolarized more effectively by heating it for three minutes and holding it for about a minute, while hot, in a solution of 10 per cent nitric acid. (*Note. Nitric acid is a strong oxidizing agent. It is also a strong acid. It will discolor and destroy clothing.*) Hold the carbon rod in a gas flame for about three minutes. The instructor will then depolarize it for you in nitric acid.

3. What depolarizer or oxidizing agent is used in the construction of dry cells? See *Practical Physics*, Millikan, Gale, and Pyle.

4. What is the voltage of an ammonium-chloride cell? The dry cell is a form of the ammonium-chloride cell. Large cells have the same voltage as small ones. See Millikan, Gale, and Pyle, *Leclanché Cell.*

5. Connect your cell in series with the cell made by some other student or with a dry cell. How many volts should two cells in series have? Refer to text.

6. Operate an electric bell by means of two liquid cells in series. What evidence have you that the voltage of two cells is able to force more current through the resistance of the bell than one?

7. Describe briefly the construction of a simple liquid cell which uses sulphuric acid as the electrolyte. Diagram it. Refer to a physics text.

8. What is meant by local action? See textbooks.

9. Diagram a dry cell and name the parts.

C. **The Dry Cell.** The dry cell is a modification of the Leclanché cell. The negative electrode is a zinc can containing a carbon rod at the center. Between the zinc and the carbon there is a damp mixture of ammonium chloride, zinc chloride, sand, manganese dioxide, etc. The manganese dioxide is a depolarizer.

The top of the can is then sealed with pitch to prevent the so-called dry cell from really becoming dry. If the pitch is cracked, or if holes are made in the zinc so that the moisture dries out, the cell becomes useless. The voltage of a dry cell remains fairly constant whether it is new or nearly discharged. The amperage will vary widely, depending upon age and usage. When a dry cell is short-circuited, the stored-up energy produces heat in the wires and in the cell. At present the dry cell has largely replaced the older forms of liquid cells.

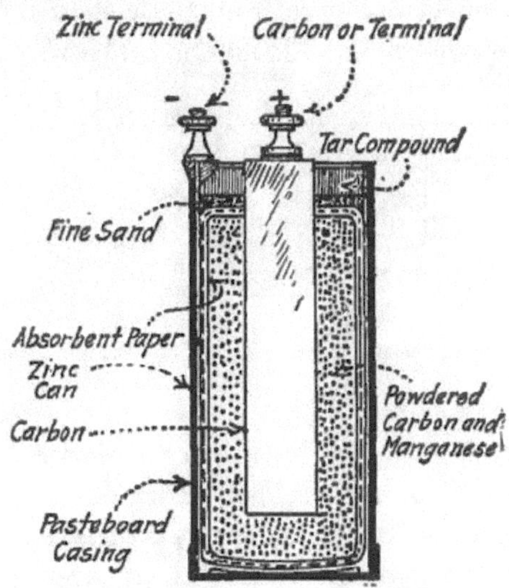

FIG. 16.—Cross-section of a dry cell.

14. INTRODUCTORY ELECTRICAL WORK—B

Measuring Volts (Pressure) and Amperes (Rate of Flow)

MATERIALS. Two dry cells; No. 24 copper wire (insulated); battery-voltmeter; 35-ampere battery ammeter; push-button.

A. **Making Measurements.** Attach two wires firmly to the binding posts of one of the cells, taking care that the two wires do not touch each other and cause a short circuit. (A short circuit would heat the wires and rapidly waste away the energy of the cell.) Attach one wire to one of the voltmeter binding posts. Connect the other wire to one side of the push-button. From the other side of the push-button connect a wire to the second post of the voltmeter. Now push the button and read the voltage of the dry cell. In the same way measure the voltage of the second cell. (*Caution. In measuring amperes, the 35-ampere ammeter must be connected in series with a push-button in order to avoid wasting the current.*) Connect one wire from the cell to the push-button and to one post of the meter. Hold the other wire firmly against the

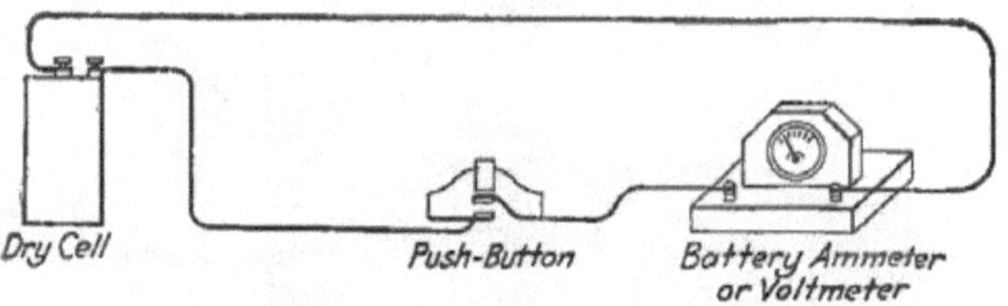

FIG. 17.—Wiring for measuring voltage or for testing the amperage of a dry cell.

other post and push the button *for a moment*. Note the total amperage output of each cell on short circuit. Connect the two cells in series according to instructor's directions, and measure the voltage, then measure the output in amperes with the 35-ampere ammeter and push-button. When you have finished working with dry cells take the wires off immediately to avoid accidently short-circuiting them. Screw the top off the push-button and examine it.

1. Make a table with two columns, one for volts and one for amperes. Record voltage and amperage output of cell No. 1, cell No. 2, the two cells in series, and three cells in series. (Note: These meters give only approximate readings.)

2. What is the correct voltage of a Leclanché cell? Same as dry cell. See *Practical Physics*, Millikan, Gale, and Pyle.

B. **Meters.** (*Caution. Sensitive voltmeters and ammeters are easily ruined by attaching them to currents of too high voltage or too high amperage.*) Expensive meters have very delicately balanced indicators. Ammeters should always be connected in series with some instrument as a lamp or motor, except in special cases like measuring the output of the dry cell with a meter of high-amperage scale.

3. What might happen to an ammeter which registers only 5 amperes (5-ampere scale) if it were attached to a new dry cell or to the 100-volt line without a lamp or some other instrument in series for resistance? A lamp or motor offers resistance and permits only a small amount of current (amperes) to flow.

4. Make a diagram showing how an ammeter should be connected with a lamp or other resistance in series to prevent ruining (short-circuiting) the ammeter.

5. How many dry cells are needed to supply 12 volts?

6. Diagram the proper number of cells in series to operate one 6-volt lamp by means of a push-button in the circuit.

7. Operate a 3-volt lamp by means of dry cells. Diagram the proper number of cells to operate two 3-volt lamps in parallel by means of a single push-button.

C. **Cells in Parallel.** For special purposes dry cells are sometimes connected in parallel (positive to positive and negative to negative). This produces the effect of a single cell of very large electrodes. The voltage is the same as that of one cell, but the amperage is increased according to the number of cells used.

7. Diagram a circuit containing three cells in parallel, operating three $1\frac{1}{2}$-volt lamps.

15. INTRODUCTORY ELECTRICAL WORK—C

Wiring and Operating a Miniature Electric Light and Power System and Measuring the Current

MATERIALS. Two ring stands; two clamps; two crossbars of wood each 5 ins. long; two dry cells; No. 24 copper wire (insulated); three 3-volt lamps; small 3-volt motor; electric bell; battery voltmeter; 35-ampere battery ammeter; push-button.

A. **Setting up a Miniature Wiring System.** Using two ring stands as supports, attach two wooden crossbars by means of clamps. See instructor's model of the apparatus. To these crossbars lead two No. 24 insulated wires, each about 1 yard long. They should be fastened to holes in the crossbars. Attach these wires to the set of two cells connected in series. Care should be taken to keep the free ends of the wires from touching each other. With a knife remove the insulation from the wires at two opposite points, and hang a 3-volt lamp across. You will find that this lamp does not let through as much current (amperes) as the cells can produce. Each lamp requires about $\frac{1}{2}$ ampere or less. The 35-ampere ammeter is not sensitive enough to measure the current used by a single small lamp.

1. How many amperes would three such lamps use? Attach three lamps in parallel on the line wires. Disconnect one of the wires at the battery and attach the ammeter in the circuit. See if three lamps cause it to register any current flow.

2. If the total output of the two cells is 15 amperes, how many such lamps could be operated at one time? Of course the battery would not last long at this rate of current consumption.

B. **Operating a Motor and a Bell.** Operate a small electric motor from your line current.

3. Connect the ammeter in series with the motor and note how much current it allows to pass through.

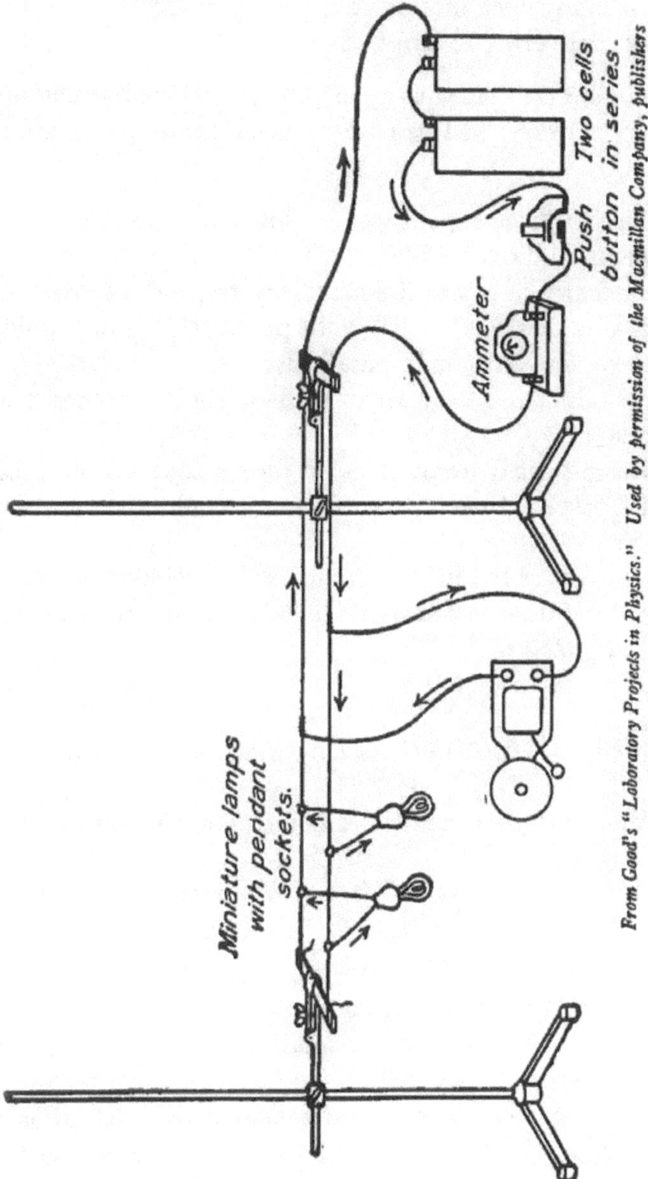

From Good's "Laboratory Projects in Physics." Used by permission of the Macmillan Company, publishers

FIG. 18.—Wiring for miniature light and power system.

4. How many such motors could be operated at one time with a set of cells delivering 10 amperes?

Attach an electric bell with a push-button to the line and operate it. An electric door bell usually requires about $\frac{1}{5}$ ampere and 3 volts.

5. Which is more expensive—to ring a bell or to light a lamp of the type used above? Why?

6. How many dry cells are necessary to produce 3-volts pressure? Six-volts pressure? Nine-volts pressure? How should they be connected—in series or in parallel?

7. How might a cell or set of cells be short-circuited and the current wasted?

8. With respect to amperes, what does a short circuit mean?

9. With respect to length of wire, how could a short circuit be avoided?

10. With respect to kind of conductor, how could a short circuit be avoided? What is meant by high-resistance wire or a high-resistance lamp?

16. INTRODUCTORY ELECTRICAL WORK—D

Electromagnets, Permanent Magnets, and the Electric Bell

MATERIALS. Two dry cells; 4 ft. No. 24 insulated wire; large iron nail; small nails; compass; steel knitting rod; push-button; electric bell.

A. **Magnets.** Wind the wire around an iron nail, making about fifteen or twenty turns, connect it in series with the push-button and note the effect on the small nails when the ends of the wire are touched to a dry cell. (*Caution. Do not let the current flow through this short wire for more than a moment, as it would soon ruin the dry cell.*) With a compass, test for N and S poles of the magnet. The south pole of the coil will attract the north pole of the compass. Reverse the direction of current by interchanging the ends of the wires on the dry cell and retest for poles.

1. How is the polarity affected by reversing the flow of current?

2. Does a soft-iron nail retain its magnetism when the current ceases?

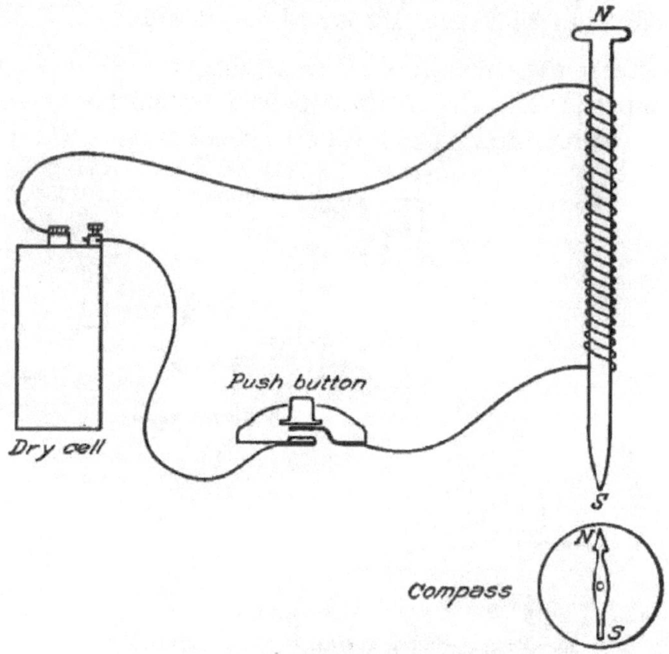

From Good's "Laboratory Projects in Physics." Used by permission of the Macmillan Company, publishers

Fig. 19.—Apparatus for the study of magnetism.

3. State the law which applies to the attraction and repulsion of poles. This law, discovered by Oersted, in 1819, has been applied in the invention of such instruments as the electric bell, telegraph, telephone, dynamo, motor, etc.

Place a hard-steel knitting rod, or old file, in a large coil and send direct current from the 110-volt line, a storage battery, or dry cells through the coil. Withdraw, and test it for magnetism.

4. What can you say of its permanency? Refer to texts.

5. Should soft iron or hard steel be used in an electro- (temporary) magnet? What would be the objection to the other?

6. The earth is a great magnet. Where are the earth's magmetic poles?

7. Distinguish between permanent magnets and electromagnets.

8. Explain what a compass is and how it works.

To increase the strength of an electromagnet, send a larger current (amperes) through the turns of wire around the bar, or keep the same current flowing and wind on more turns. The product

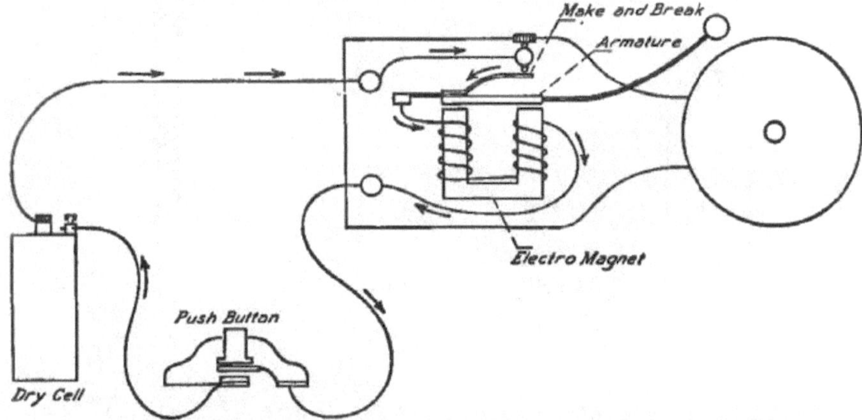

From Good's "Laboratory Projects in Physics." Used by permission of the Macmillan Company, publishers

FIG. 20.—Path of electric current in operating an electric bell.

of the amperes (current) and the number of turns determine the magnetizing strength of the coil. Since electromagnets are more powerful than permanent magnets and since their magnetism can be quickly destroyed, they have been given a great many practical applications, such as electric bells, electric motors, electric generators, induction coils, telegraph, telephone, and wireless instruments. Electromagnetic cranes are used in lifting heavy masses of iron in steel mills and in the manufacture of nails, bolts, etc. A large magnetic crane will lift two tons of iron at one time.

B. **The Electric Bell.** In the vibrating bell, when the circuit is closed by pushing the button, there is an arrangement in the bell which alternately closes and opens the circuit.

9. Diagram a bell, indicating the path of current by means of arrows. The path of the current is not exactly the same in all bells. See *Practical Physics*, Millikan, Gale, and Pyle.

10. What caused the tapper to move toward the bell?

11. What stops the flow of the current?

12. What causes the tapper to move away from the bell?

13. Diagram a circuit showing a battery, a push-button, and a bell.

14. Diagram a battery and one push-button operating two bells. The bells should be attached in parallel.

17. THE ELECTRIC MOTOR

The Construction and Operation of an Electric Motor

MATERIALS. St. Louis motor; two dry cells; No. 24 wire; 35-ampere battery ammeter.

One form of simple electric motor consists of two electromagnets —one stationary and the other so arranged that it revolves in the magnetic field of the stationary coil. A device known as a commutator reverses the direction of flow through the revolving coil each half turn. The principal parts of a motor are: field magnet, field coil, armature (revolving coil), commutator, and brushes.

A. **Motor Operated with Permanent Field Magnet.** Remove the field-coil attachment from the base board and lay it aside. Using the two permanent bar magnets for the field magnetism, attach wires from one dry cell to the upper binding posts, causing the armature to rotate.

1. Name two of the essential parts of the motor through which the current passes before it reaches the armature coil.

2. What causes the armature coil to become magnetized?

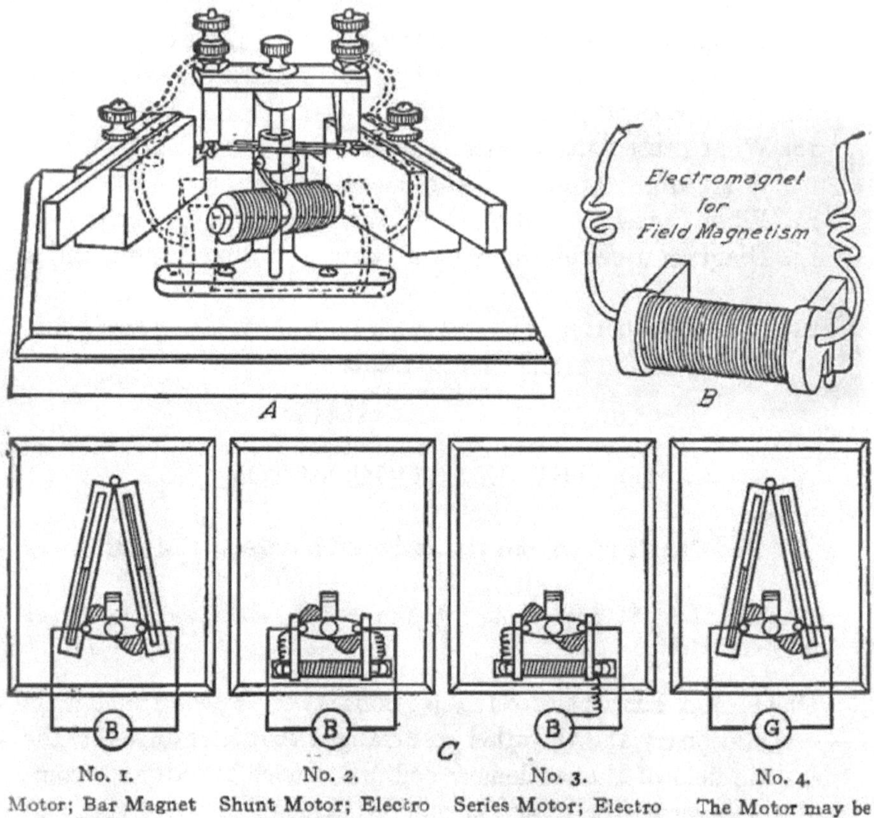

From Good's "Laboratory Projects in Physics." Used by permission of the Macmillan Company, publishers

Fig. 21.—A simple electric motor.

3. When the current is reversed through an electromagnet what happens to its poles?

4. For what part of a revolution does the current flow in one direction through this armature coil?

5. How many times during each revolution are the poles of this armature reversed?

6. State the law which applies to the attraction and repulsion of magnetic poles.

7. What should happen with regard to the direction of current flow when the south pole of the armature comes nearest to the north pole of the field?

8. What effect upon the direction of rotation of this motor is caused by reversing the field poles?

9. Reverse the battery wires at the brush posts of the motor. What effect has this upon the direction of rotation?

10. What effect upon the speed of the armature is produced by turning the brush frame out of its normal position?

11. If the field poles are both north or both south (like poles), what is the effect upon the rotation of the armature?

B. **Motor Operated with Electromagnet for its Field.** Push the permanent bar magnets aside and place the electromagnet coil in position to furnish the field magnetism. Connect wires so that current from two dry cells passes first through the armature coil and then through the field coil and back to the dry cells. This represents a series-wound motor.

12. Diagram a series-wound motor. Observe the illustrations and refer to text on wiring of motors or generators.

13. Connect a battery ammeter and measure the current which the pressure of two dry cells sends through the motor.

14. Two dry cells in series have approximately 3 volts pressure. What is the resistance of this motor in ohms? While measuring the current for resistance do not let the armature rotate. Hold it. Apply Ohm's Law (volts divided by ohms equal amperes).

15. This motor would be ruined if attached directly to the 110-volt lines. With its resistance known, calculate by Ohm's Law how many amperes would pass through it if it were attached without additional resistance to the 110-volt line.

16. Operate this motor with shunt wiring. Have the wiring approved by the instructor. Diagram a motor wired in shunt. See *Practical Physics*, Black and Davis. Use diagram for shunt generator, omitting lamps.

18. THE ELECTRIC GENERATOR (DYNAMO)

The Construction and Operation of an Electric Generator

NOTE. It is preferable to take the experiment dealing with the "Electric Motor" preliminary to this experiment. Handle apparatus carefully.

MATERIALS. Small generator, operated by hand power (L. E. Knott hand-power dissectible dynamo and motor); small lamp; battery ammeter; battery voltmeter; electric bell; small motor; telephone magneto generator. (Part of this apparatus must be obtained from the instructor.)

A. **Explanation and Operation.** In construction the simple generator is a device for revolving a coil of wire between the poles of a strong electromagnet. When a magnet moves into a coil or away from it, a current is generated in the coil. Or if a coil revolves in the presence of a magnet, a current is generated in the coil. The coil cuts the lines of force produced by the magnet. (The wires leading from the coil must be connected to complete a circuit.)

Operate the small hand-power generator. Connect wires to it, causing it to ring a bell, light a small lamp, and run a small motor.

1. Attach a battery voltmeter to the terminals and measure its voltage at your maximum speed.

2. Attach a battery ammeter in series with a small motor, and measure the amperage which passes through it at your maximum speed.

3. How does varying the speed affect the voltage? As the voltage increases the amperage also increases through a given resistance.

4. Make two simple diagrams of generators showing series winding and shunt winding. See *Practical Physics*, Black and Davis.

5. If a generator armature contains a commutator, will the current be direct or alternating?

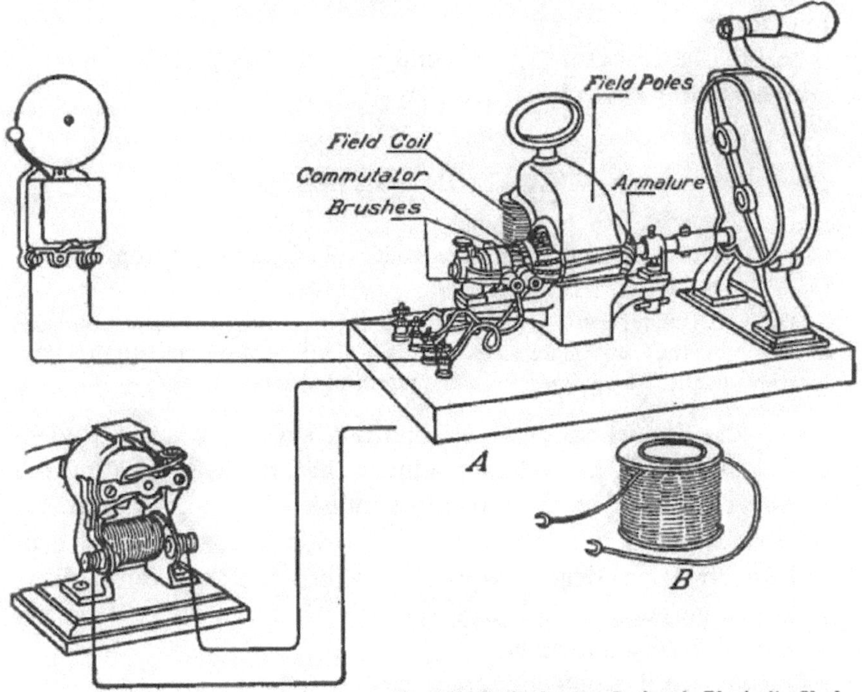

From Good's "Laboratory Projects in Physics." Used by permission of the Macmillan Company, publishers

FIG. 22.—An electric generator.

6. What is the function of the field coils of an electric generator?

7. Of what material are the brushes in this small generator made? in large generators and motors?

8. How does a generator get its field magnetism? Refer to texts. At the beginning a very small amount of residual magnetism remains in the magnets from the last running to start the voltage in the armature, which in turn starts a small current.

B. **Telephone Magneto Generator.** Operate this generator and attach a small lamp. This device is sometimes used on telephone instruments for the purpose of ringing up the party at the other end of the line.

9. How does its field magnet differ from that of the regular generator?
10. If the armature shaft contains rings in place of a commutator, what kind of current does it deliver?

19. IGNITION SYSTEMS—A

Setting up and Operating a Simple Ignition System

MATERIALS. Four dry cells; insulated wires; vibrating induction coil; metal-ring stand; automobile spark plug. (Part of the apparatus for this experiment must be obtained from the instructor.)

A. **The Induction Coil.** An ignition system in a gas engine, or an automobile, is used to produce a hot spark for igniting the explosive mixture in the engine cylinder. This may be accomplished by sending a 6-volt current through an induction coil, and thereby increasing the voltage to 10,000 or 15,000 volts. This high-voltage current will pass through air for a short distance, producing a very hot spark.

Operate a vibrating induction coil as follows: Attach a short wire from one of the secondary terminals of the induction coil to within ¼ inch of the other secondary terminal, but not touching it. This ¼-inch opening will form the spark gap. An induction coil should not be operated with the spark gap too wide, as this may puncture the insulation of the secondary coil and ruin it. Connect four dry cells in series. (*Caution. The current from the secondary terminals of an induction coil is dangerous. Keep away from the secondary wires when the batteries are attached.*) Attach one wire from the dry cells to one of the primary terminals of the induction coil. Touch the other wire from the dry cells to the other primary terminal of the induction coil. A spark should jump across the spark gap of the secondary terminals. Do not handle the induction coil without first disconnecting the dry cells.

1. Diagram an induction coil. See Fig. 33.

2. Should the current which passes through the primary

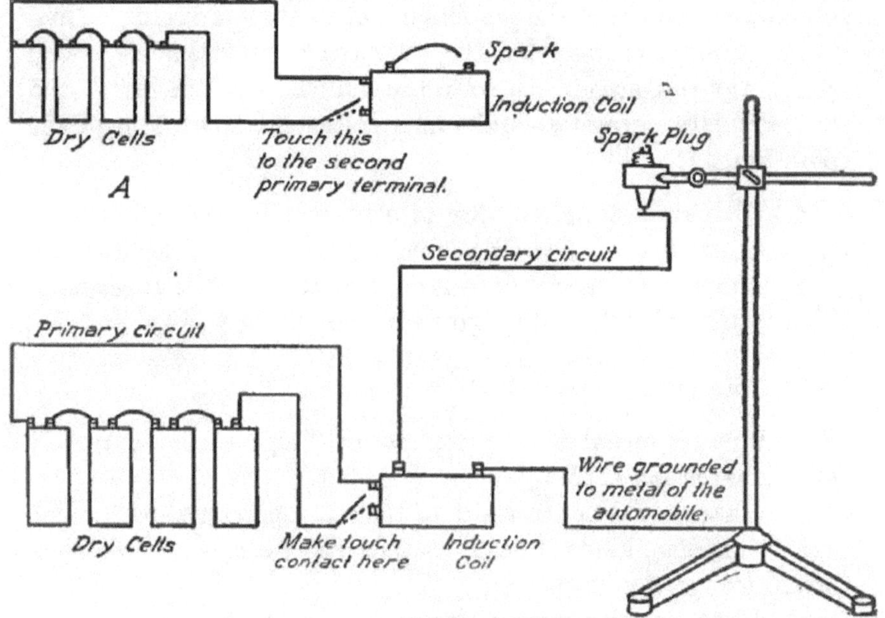

From Good's "Laboratory Projects in Physics." Used by permission of the Macmillan Company, publishers

FIG. 23.—Simple ignition system containing primary and secondary circuits.

winding of this type of coil be a continuous flow or an intermittent flow?

3. Explain the purpose of the vibrator. If the vibrator does not operate, it may need some adjustment. Consult the instructor.

4. What pulls the vibrator toward the coil? What draws it back?

5. What is a condenser made of? What is its function? In

automobile ignition systems, the timer usually serves the purpose of the vibrator and the induction coil does not contain a vibrator.

B. **The Secondary Circuit—Spark Plug.** Disconnect the batteries, temporarily, from the induction coil. Remove the wire from the secondary terminals. Fasten an automobile spark plug to the clamp of the ring stand. Connect a well-insulated wire from one secondary terminal of the induction coil to the spark plug. Connect a second wire from the other secondary terminal to any metal part of the ring stand. Operate the induction coil as before and the secondary current should jump across the spark gap of the spark plug.

6. Diagram a sectional view of a spark plug and tell of what materials it is made. See *The Gasoline Automobile, Motor Vehicles.*
7. The secondary circuit is grounded through the ring stand. What is meant by the term "grounded circuit"?

C. **Reference Work.**

8. What is meant by the expressions "high-tension current" and "low-tension current"?
9. What should be the width of the spark gap on a spark plug?
10. Name two kinds of batteries that may be used for producing current for ignition purposes.
11. What are two common classes of magnetos?
12. How can the spark plug of an automobile be tested to insure that it sparks?
13. State three possible causes of trouble in the electric circuits.

20. IGNITION SYSTEMS—B

Operation of Automobile Ignition Systems

MATERIALS. Four dry cells; vibrating induction coil; four metal-ring stands; four spark plugs; wooden block with four binding posts; non-vibrating induction coil (make-and-break coil). (Part of the apparatus for this experiment must be obtained from the instructor.)

A. **Automobile Ignition System.** Attach four spark plugs to four ring stands. Connect the four stands by means of a wire, and extend this wire to one terminal of the induction coil. From the four spark plugs lead four well-insulated wires to four binding-posts placed near the corners of a square wooden block. Attach a well-insulated wire to the second terminal of the vibrating induction coil. Insulate this wire by pulling a piece of rubber tubing over it. (*Caution. The secondary current is dangerous. Keep away from the secondary wires when the batteries are attached.*) When this wire is placed in contact with any one of the posts on the wooden block, you should get a spark at the spark plug which that post controls. This block with the four posts represents the " distributor " of a four-cylinder automobile ignition system.

The closing of the battery circuit (primary circuit) by touching one wire to one of the primary terminals of the induction coil represents the " timer " of an automobile ignition system.

Automobiles, as a rule, do not have vibrating coils. The timer makes and breaks the primary circuit, serving the purposes of the vibrator. The Ford ignition system is an exception. The Ford car is provided with four vibrating coils, one for each cylinder.

In many of the common types of cars the low-voltage current supply for operating the induction coil is taken from the storage battery.

1. Diagram the apparatus used above, showing dry cells, induction coil, spark plugs, and distributor.

2. State the two possible sequences of firing for four-cylinder engines. See *Motor Vehicles.*

3. What is the purpose of the ignition switch on the instrument board of an automobile?

4. What is the purpose of the distributor?

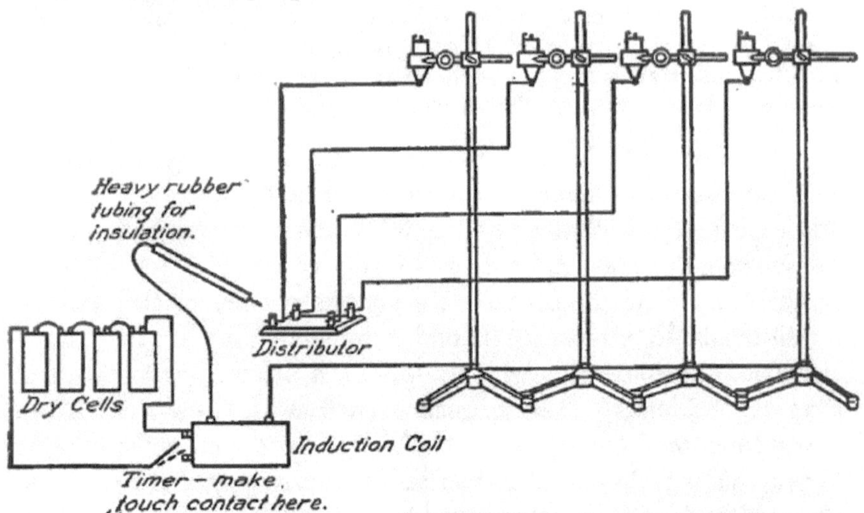

From Good's "Laboratory Projects in Physics." Used by permission of the Macmillan Company, publishers

FIG. 24.—Ignition system, illustrating the operation of the timer and the distributor of an automobile.

B. **Make-and-break Ignition.** Some gas engines are operated by a "make-and-break" spark (wipe spark). Connect up four dry cells. Connect a wire from one terminal of the battery to a simple "make-and-break" coil. This device consists of a coil of wire wound around an iron core. Slip a heavy rubber tube over the second wire from the battery for insulation. Touch the second terminal of the make-and-break coil with the second wire from the battery, and pull it quickly away. Use one hand only, to avoid a shock. A hot spark will occur at the time of break, due to the self-induced voltage in the coil. If this make-and-break occurs in the cylinder of an engine, the spark may be used for ignition.

5. Diagram a make-and-break ignition system. See *The Gasoline Automobile.*

C. **Magneto Generators.** Magnetos are sometimes employed as sources of current for ignition. These generators take the place of the battery. They are either of the high-tension or the low-tension types. The low-tension magneto requires a separate induction coil. The high-tension magneto is constructed with the induction coil in the magneto.

D. **Reference Work.** *The Gasoline Automobile.*

6. Make a diagram showing the main parts of a typical ignition system, including induction coil and distributor.

7. State at least five possible causes of failure of an ignition system to produce a spark.

21. STORAGE BATTERY—A

The Construction and Operation of a Simple Lead-storage Cell

MATERIALS. Simple storage cell; dilute solution of common salt; battery voltmeter: electric bell; 2-volt lamp; small 2-volt motor; lamp board and 1-ampere lamp; 110-volt or lower voltage direct current.

Caution. Sulphuric acid will destroy clothing and cause burns. Handle with extreme care.

A. Make a simple storage cell by filling a battery jar three-fourths full of a 20 per cent solution of sulphuric acid. Suspend in it two plates of ordinary sheet lead by folding the lead plates over the edges of the jar. With a 1-ampere lamp as rheostat, prepare to send a 110-volt direct current through the cell or to send a direct current from a small generator. (*Caution. Do not connect the cell directly to the line wires without resistance, as this would blow out the fuse.*) Test the charging current with a salt solution (a quarter teaspoonful in a tumblerful of water) to find which terminal is negative. In making this test attach the lamp in series with one wire to insure against a short circuit if the wires should accidently touch in the salt solution. The negative terminal gives off more bubbles. Connect the brown-coated plate (positive) to the positive terminal of the line. In charging, connect positive to positive and negative to negative.

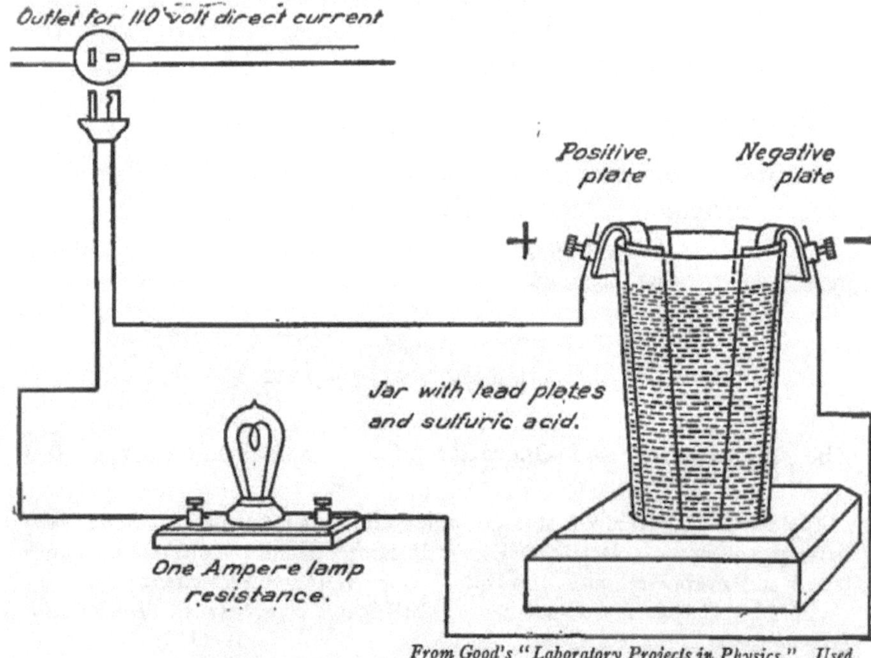

From Good's "Laboratory Projects in Physics." Used by permission of the Macmillan Company, publishers

FIG. 25.—Wiring scheme for charging a simple storage battery.

The charging current should pass through the cell from positive to negative. Hydrogen is set free at the negative plate and oxygen at the positive (electrolysis). The oxygen, instead of escaping into the air, attacks the lead, forming a brown coat of lead peroxide, PbO_2. When the cell is charged, the positive plate is coated with lead peroxide and the negative plate of pure lead act like the positive and negative plates of any simple liquid cell.

Allow the current to pass through this cell for fifteen minutes (Read Black and Davis on the storage battery.) Disconnect from the charging lines and test the pressure with a voltmeter. (*Caution. Do not connect an ammeter to a storage battery without some resistance such as a motor or a lamp in series with the meter, as this might ruin both the ammeter and the battery.*)

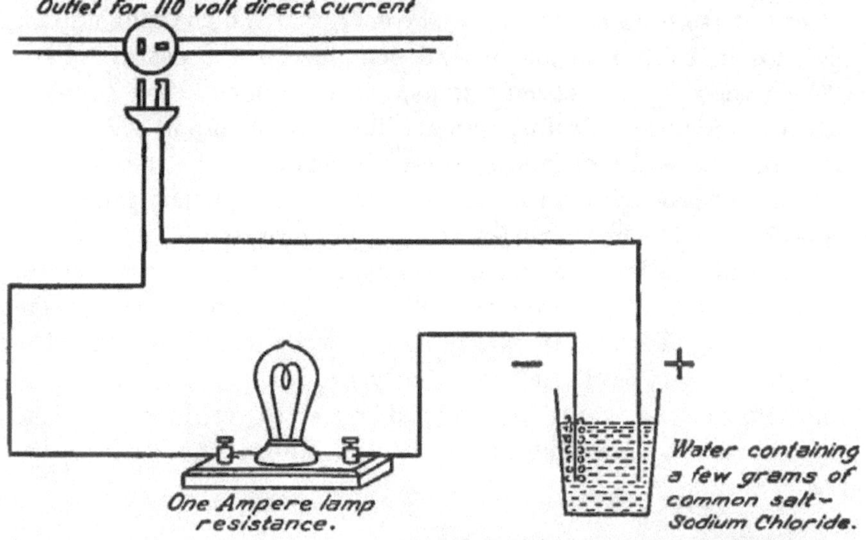

From Good's "Laboratory Projects in Physics." Used by permission of the Macmillan Company, publishers

FIG. 26.—Apparatus for determining which terminal of a supply line is positive.

1. What is the voltage of a lead-storage cell? See texts.

2. Ring an electric bell. Make a diagram of the apparatus with parts labeled.

3 Operate a small motor and measure the amperage.

4. What happens to a storage battery if the wires are connected without resistance (some suitable lamp or motor)?

B. **Chemical Reaction.** Disregarding intermediate steps in the chemical reaction, we may represent the operation as follows:

Charged Condition				Discharged Condition		
Pos. Plate	Elec- trolyte	Neg. Plate		Pos. Plate	Elec- trolyte	Neg. Plate
PbO_2 +	$2H_2SO_4$ +	Pb	$\rightleftarrows$	$PbSO_4$ +	$2H_2O$ +	$PbSO_4$

The reaction goes in the opposite direction when a current is reversed through the cell in the operation of charging it. The cell does not store up electricity. The energy of the charging current is used in the formation of lead peroxide on the positive plate. When the charging current stops, the two plates, on account of their different chemical nature, act like a simple liquid cell, which, on account of the chemical difference between the two plates, is capable of producing a reaction with the electrolyte and generating a current. The hydrogen ions of the sulphuric acid unite with the oxygen of the lead peroxide, forming water, and SO_4 ions go to produce lead sulphate on both plates. Thus on full charge the sulphuric acid is concentrated and on discharge it is dilute. The specific gravity is, therefore, a fairly good test of the charged or discharged condition of the cell. The electrolyte, however, must be kept full by the addition of distilled water, since evaporation reduces it.

Reference Work. *Practical Physics*, Black and Davis.

5. When a storage battery is discharged what chemical compound covers the plates?
6. What are some disadvantages of a lead storage battery?
7. What efficiency is obtained from a battery in good condition?
8. Mention three uses for storage batteries.
9. In the Edison storage battery what are the plates composed of and what electrolyte is used?

22. AUTOMOBILE ELECTRIC CIRCUITS—A

Storage-battery Charging and Ignition Circuits

NOTE. The experiments, Ignition Systems—A and Ignition Systems—B should precede this experiment.

MATERIALS. Automobile with storage battery, ignition, starting and lighting circuits.

A. **The Charging Circuit.** The generator is used for charging the storage battery. The current which it produces passes through the ammeter, thus indicating at all times the amount of charging current which the storage battery receives.

1. By means of the wires, beginning at the generator, trace the circuit which carries current through the storage battery, including the ammeter on the instrument board.
2. Make a simple wiring diagram showing the positions of generator, ammeter, and storage battery. Have this work approved by the instructor.

B. **The Ignition Circuit—A.** In starting the engine the ignition current in many cars is supplied by the storage battery. This current is carried to the timer and the induction coil which produces a high-tension current for operating the spark plugs. The timer is a device for making and breaking the primary circuit of the induction coil comparable in effect to the vibrator on a vibrating coil. It serves to make and break the flow of current through the primary coil of the induction coil. These pulses induce a high-voltage current in the secondary coil which is connected to the spark plugs.

3. By means of the wires trace and record the battery ignition circuit, beginning with the positive side of the storage battery, including the ammeter, the ignition switch, the timer, and the primary circuit of the induction coil.

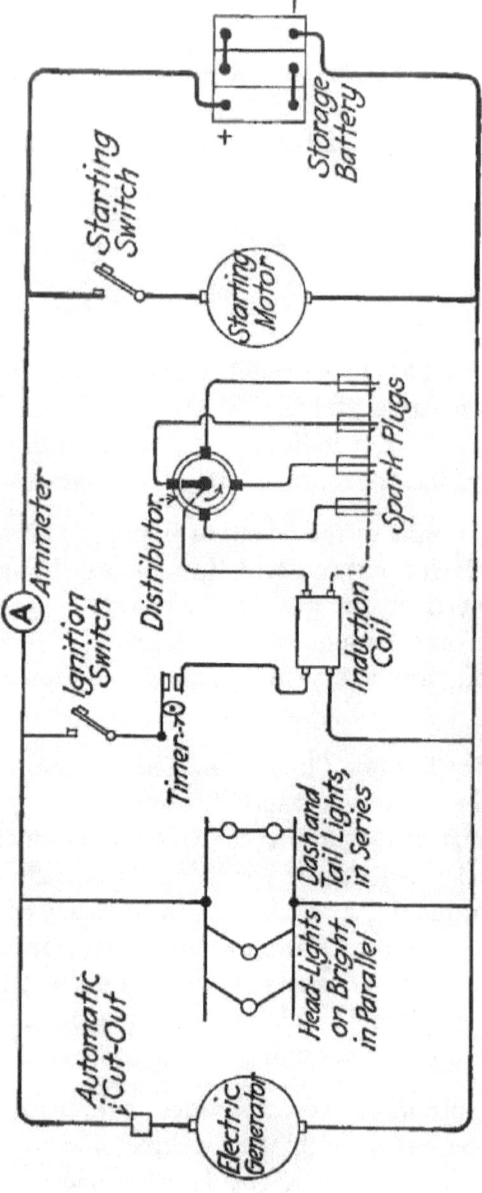

FIG. 27.—Wiring circuits of a typical automobile.

4. Make a simple wiring diagram of a battery ignition circuit showing the positions of the above parts. See diagrams in *The Gasoline Automobile*, chapter on Battery Ignition Systems.

The secondary circuit of the induction coil leads back to the distributor. Here the high-tension current is sent out to each spark plug at the proper time for the explosion. Note that the secondary circuit of the induction coil is represented by only one heavily insulated wire. Instead of a return wire from the outside of the plug to the induction coil the metal of the car serves to bring this current back. This is known as a grounded circuit.

5. In the ignition circuit what is the function of the ignition switch located on the instrument board?

6. What is the function of the induction coil?

7. Diagram a timer mechanism, showing contact arm, cam, condenser, and breaker points.

8. Explain the purpose of each of these parts of the timer. See *The Gasoline Automobile.*

23. AUTOMOBILE ELECTRIC CIRCUITS—B

Storage Battery Ignition, Lighting, and Starting Circuits

A. **Ignition Circuit. Ignition Current from the Generator.** When the car is running faster than 8 or 10 miles an hour the generator delivers a current with voltage greater than that of the storage battery. This overcomes the battery pressure and forces current back into the storage battery charging it. At the same time, at speeds above 8 or 10 miles per hour, the generator supplies part of its current to the induction coil for ignition.

Note that the wiring scheme makes this possible. Accordingly, when the engine attains the proper speed, the ammeter no longer indicates that the storage battery is discharging, but the indicator moves over to the charging side, showing that current is flowing through the instrument in the opposite direction.

Beginning at the generator, by means of the wires trace the path of current which the generator supplies for operating the primary circuit of the induction coil. This circuit should include generator, ignition switch, timer, and primary of the induction coil.

1. Make a wiring diagram showing the relative positions of the different units of this circuit. Include, also, the ammeter and the storage battery in relation to the generator ignition circuit.

2. Does current in this generator ignition circuit flow through the ammeter?

B. **Lighting Circuits.** Assume that lighting current is obtained from the storage battery. This circuit is carried to the lighting switch on the instrument board from which point it is distributed to the lighting circuits.

3. Beginning at the storage battery trace the wiring to the

lighting switch on the instrument board and return to the storage battery. Make a diagram with proper instruments included.

4. Beginning at the lighting switch, diagram a wiring scheme which represents the headlight circuit when the lamps are operated " bright " (lamps in parallel).

5. Diagram a headlight wiring circuit from the lighting switch when the lamps are lighted " dim " (lamps in series).

6. What is the voltage of the storage battery? (Each lead cell gives approximately two volts.)

7. When does more current flow through the lamps, in series or in parallel?

8. Which have the greater resistance, two lamps in series or two lamps in parallel?

9. What voltage lamps are used in the headlights? What would be the effects if lamps of double this voltage or half this voltage were used?

10. If one headlight burns out, can the other one be operated,— (*a*) " dim "? (*b*) " bright " ? Explain.

11. Diagram the circuit which operates the instrument board light; and the tail light.

12. What is the voltage of each of these lights?

13. Why are they connected in series?

C. **The Electric Starting System.**

14. Diagram the starting circuit with necessary parts represented.

15. Why are the wires which lead from the battery to the starting motor very heavy? With a 6-volt battery about what amperage is required to operate a starting motor?

24. ENGINE COOLING SYSTEMS—B

Pump Systems, the Franklin Air-Cooled System, Troubles and Repairs

MATERIALS. Automobile chassis, reference books.

A. **Pump System of Cooling.** A more positive means of circulation in the cooling system is obtained in many of the higher-priced cars by using a pump in the circulating system.

1. Which system—pump or thermo-siphon—is more likely to permit the water surrounding the cylinders to become (*a*) too hot? (*b*) too cold?

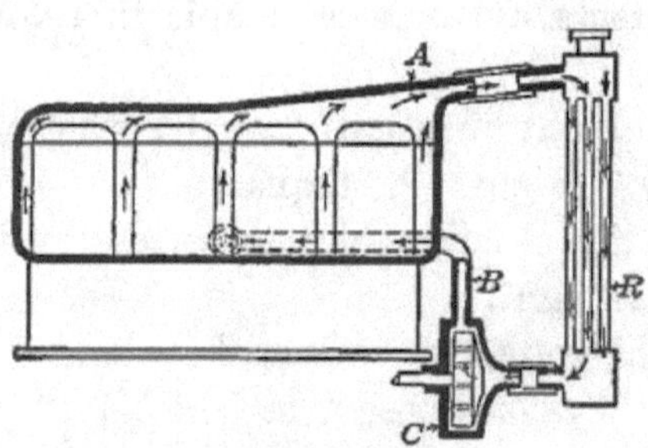

FIG. 28.—Pump system.

2. What type of pump is most common in pump systems of circulation?

3. Does a pump-feed system usually have smaller or larger pipes than a thermo-siphon system? Why?

4. Explain the fact that an engine works more efficiently when the temperature of the water in the water jacket is above 160° F.

5. What is the function of a thermostatic valve on a water-cooling system? Name one make of car that is equipped with a thermostatic valve.

B. **The Franklin Air-cooling System.**

6. Describe briefly the Franklin cooling system. See *The Gasoline Automobile.*

C. **Anti-freezing Mixtures.**

7. List the characteristics of an ideal anti-freezing compound. Does any specific mixture or solution possess all of these characteristics? See *The Gasoline Automobile.*

8. Explain the method of making up anti-freezing mixtures to withstand a temperature of zero F. from (*a*) calcium chloride; (*b*) denatured alcohol; (*c*) alcohol and glycerine solutions.

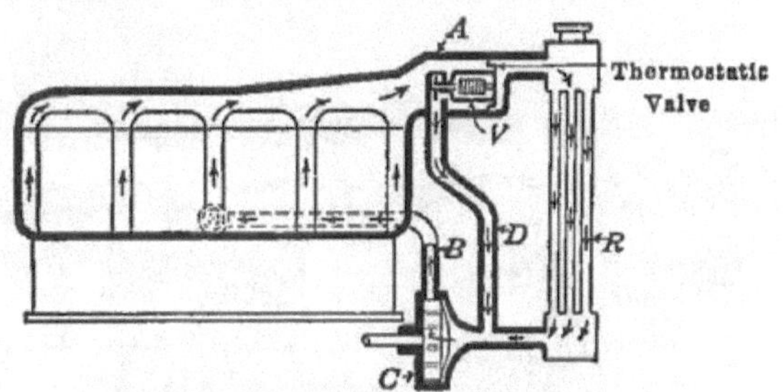

FIG. 29.—Pump system with thermostatic valve.

D. **Troubles and Remedies.**

9. Name three possible causes for water boiling in a cooling system. If the water boils, stop the engine immediately and find the cause.

10. How may sediment be removed from a cooling system? See *The Gasoline Automobile*, Cooling Troubles.

11. How may the water be kept at the efficient operating temperature in winter weather?

A radiator may feel warm at the top and be freezing below. If the tubes are frozen at the bottom, the radiator should be covered with a blanket and the engine should be run slowly until the tubes thaw out.

Leaky radiators may sometimes be repaired temporarily with such substances as sealing wax, tire putty and plaster of Paris.

25. ENGINE-OILING SYSTEMS—B

Types of Oiling Systems, Troubles, and Adjustments

MATERIALS. Automobile chassis and reference books.

The cylinders of the automobile power plant are the most difficult parts of the mechanism to lubricate on account of their location, variations in speed, and the great heat generated by the

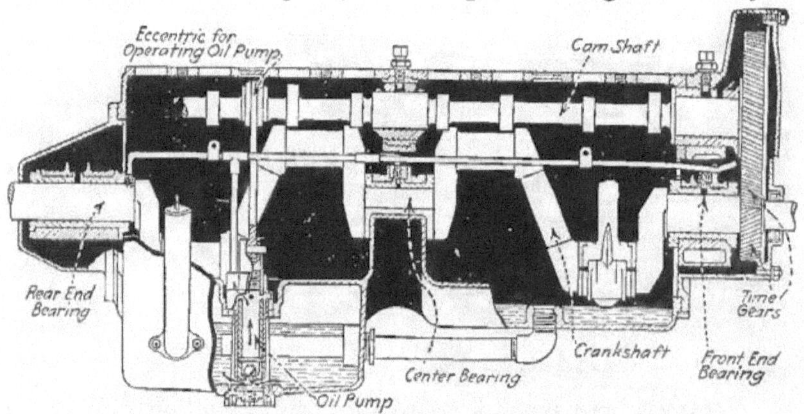

FIG. 30.—Splash system of oiling with circulating pump.

explosion of the gas. There is a possibility of excessive or insufficient oiling as well as a possibility of a lack of uniformity of oil distribution to the different cylinders. In order to provide proper lubrication under varying conditions a number of special oiling systems are in common use.

A. **Types of Oiling Systems.**

1. Name three types of splash systems. See Dyke. How do they differ?

2. What kind of lubrication system does the laboratory engine have? Describe it.

3. Name five makes of car which have circulating splash oiling systems. See Dyke, Specifications of Leading Cars.

4. Under what conditions of operation of an automobile on the road is uniformity of oil distribution difficult to maintain? See Dyke.

5. What system of lubrication is unaffected by the above conditions of operation?

6. Does the presence of an oil indicator on the dash of an automobile necessarily mean that the oiling system used is a "force-feed" system? What kind of system might it be?

7. Describe briefly the operation of the "full-force-feed" system of lubrication. Name one make of car which uses this system. See Dyke.

B. **Troubles and Adjustments.**

8. What trouble might occur in a "force-feed" system, causing it to fail to operate? What harm would result thereby?

9. Of what practical use is an oil-pressure gauge? Would an excessive oil pressure mean that the engine is getting too much oil?

10. What trouble may result (*a*) if an engine is not getting enough oil? (*b*) if it gets too much oil?

11. State the probable cause of an excessive amount of oil in the combustion chamber. Are old or new cylinders and pistons likely to have this trouble?

12. What is probably the cause if the exhaust smoke is (*a*) white or blue, (*b*) black?

13. What kind of engine oil should be used in an air-cooled engine or in an engine with loose pistons and rings?

26. LUBRICATION—TRANSMISSION AND CHASSIS

MATERIALS. Automobile chassis and reference books. Use the instruction book for the car with lubrication chart and refer to textbooks.

A. **The Clutch.** Some clutches are constructed to operate in oil, others to run dry. Cone clutches usually run dry.

1. What kind of lubricant causes wet clutches to slip? How can this trouble be remedied? See *The Gasoline Automobile.*

B. **The Change Gears.**

2. Should the lubricant be stiff grease or heavy fluid grease? Why? See *The Gasoline Automobile.*
3. How frequently should the gear box be cleaned out and refilled with new lubricant?
4. Parts of the gears in the form of chips sometimes break off and fall to the bottom of the gear case. What damage might result from using a very stiff grease instead of a semi-fluid grease?
5. How deep should the oil stand in the transmission case? See *Instruction Book.*

C. **The Universal Joint.**

6. Describe the provision for lubrication and state the type of lubricant used.

D. **The Differential and the Rear Axle.**

7. Why are semi-solid oils commonly used in the rear-axle housing. See *The Gasoline Automobile.*
8. Examine the rear axle of the Ford. State (*a*) the kind of oil required, (*b*) the amount, (*c*) how it is put in.
9. Examine the rear axle of one larger automobile. State (*a*) kind of oil required, (*b*) the amount, (*c*) what provisions are made for taking out old oil and replacing it with new.
10. How frequently should wheel bearings and the differential

be repacked with oil? If a differential chips or is badly worn, small pieces of steel may lodge in the oil.

11. What prevents grease from working out and water and sand from working into the rear-axle housing?

12. If old oil is not removed from a rear-axle housing before adding new oil, what effect does continued use have upon the old oil?

D. **Chassis.** See *Instruction Book.*

13. What parts on the front axle require lubrication?

14. How are the front wheels supplied with oil?

15. What parts of the control system require oil?

16. Why do springs need lubrication? How are they lubricated? See *The Gasoline Automobile.*

27. FRONT AXLES

Axles, Steering Adjustments, and Alignment of Wheels

MATERIALS. Automobile chassis; ball of cord; rule; reference books.

In order to insure safety the front-axle assembly and steering mechanism should be inspected frequently and adjusted when necessary. It is the function of the steering knuckle and the wheel bearings to carry the entire weight of the front of the car and to withstand hard knocks and strains. These parts, therefore, should be kept well lubricated to prevent excessive wear.

Jack up the front wheels for making a study of this mechanism.

A. **The Steering Mechanism.**

1. Explain the operation of the steering knuckle.

2. Shake front wheels vigorously. If they give evidence of play or lost motion due to wear, at what points is this wear likely to be found?

3. What is the name of the rod which connects the two steering knuckles?

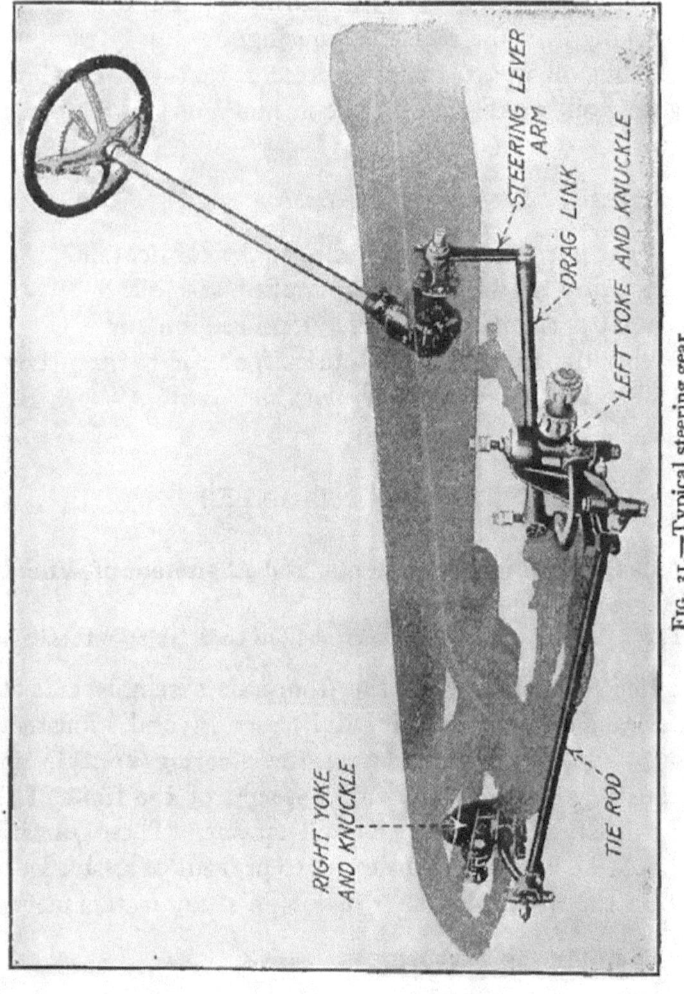

Fig. 31.—Typical steering gear.

4. If this rod should break when the car is in operation, what would the wheels do?

5. What is the function of (*a*) the steering-knuckle pin, (*b*) the

steering yoke, (*c*) the spindle, (*e*) the retention nut, (*f*) roller bearings?

B. **Wheel Alignment.** Place a chair behind one rear wheel and another chair in front of the front wheel on the same side of the car. Tie the end of a long piece of cord to the chair at the rear at a point just above the rear hub. Stretch the string to the chair in front of the front wheel and tie it at a point so that it stretches tight just above the front hub. Move the chairs so that the string just barely touches the sides of the rear wheel. Turn the front wheel so that the string just barely touches the sides of the front wheel. Now go to the opposite side of the car and sight along the line of the front and rear wheels.

6. On the opposite side does the front wheel stand in the same direction as the rear wheel? How does it stand?

7. What is this adjustment of the front wheels called? See *The Gasoline Automobile*—Alignment of Wheels.

8. How much should the two wheels vary from the parallel position?

Without changing the position of the front wheels move the chairs and the string to the opposite side of the car. Again move the string gently till it just barely touches the sides of the rear wheel and the front wheel just above the hub. Now measure how far the front edge of the front wheel is from the string.

9. How much do these wheels "toe in" or "gather"? (The wheels should run true if this method is used.)

10. If the gather is incorrect take two wrenches and reset the adjustable yoke at the one end of the tie rod. Adjust the wheels so that the gather is correct. If the gather is correct at the beginning, set it so that it is incorrect by one-half inch. Make certain to replace all cotter pins. Have this work approved by the instructor. On the report sheet describe your procedure.

11. Describe another method of measuring "toe in." See Dyke.

12. What is the reason for setting wheels with " toe in " or " gather " ?

13. What is meant by " camber " ?

14. How much camber is commonly given to wheels?

15. Explain why wheels are cambered.

28. REAR AXLES

MATERIALS. Demonstration Ford rear axle mounted on a wooden stand in the laboratory.

Remove the nuts which hold the two halves of the differential housing of the Ford rear axle and examine the differential mechanism and the axle shaft. Follow instructions given in the *Ford Manual* and in *The Model T Ford Car.* Examine illustrations in the *Ford Manual.*

A. **The Ford Rear Axle.**

1. Is the Ford axle a live axle or a dead axle? See *The Gasoline Automobile.*

2. Is this a simple, semi-floating, three-quarter-floating, or full-floating rear axle? Explain.

3. How many roller bearings has the Ford rear axle? Where are they located? See Fig. 71.

4. Which of the roller bearings carry the weight of the car?

5. What kind of bearings in the differential housing carry the end of the drive shaft?

6. What do the others carry?

7. What is the function of the radius rods? If one radius rod is bent how is the rear axle affected?

8. To what is the rear wheel attached? How is this attachment made?

9. To what is the castle or retention nut attached?

10. What does the drive-shaft pinion operate?

11. State the function of (*a*) the axle housing cap, (*b*) a thrust washer.

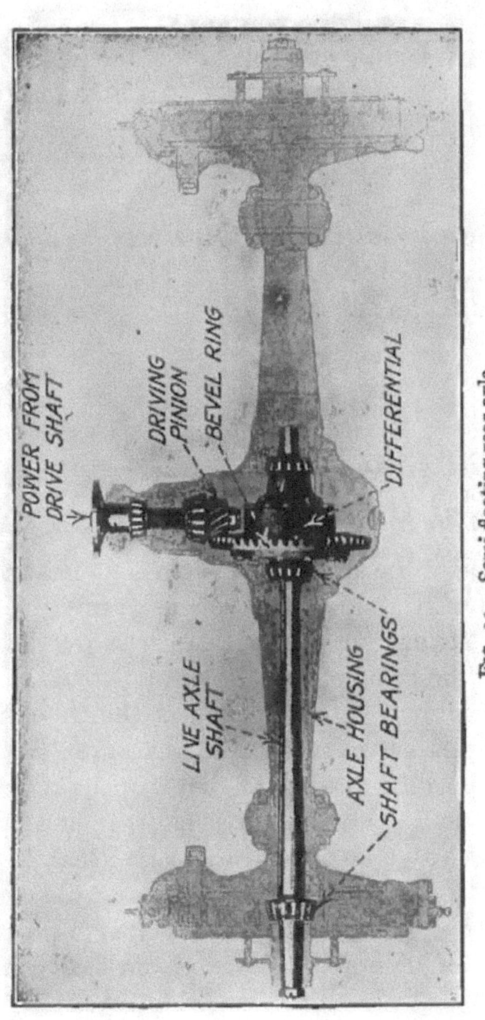

Fig. 32.—Semi-floating rear axle.

12. How is the Ford rear axle lubricated and what kind of lubrication is used?

B. **Rear Axles,—Other Types.**

13. Examine an illustration of a *full-floating* rear axle. See *Motor Vehicles.* In this type of construction does the weight rest upon the axle shaft as in the Ford or upon the axle housing?

14. In the *full-floating* rear axle how is the power for driving the rear wheel transmitted from the axle shaft to the wheel?

15. Examine an illustration of the *three-quarter-floating* type of rear axle. How does this construction differ from the *full-floating* type?

16. Examine an illustration of the *semi-floating* type. What supports the weight of the machine in this type?

17. To what is the hub fastened in the semi-floating type?

29. VALVE MECHANISMS—A

Removing a Valve, Its Characteristics and Function

MATERIALS. Ford engine; valve spring compressor; valve spring tools.

The operation of the automobile engine requires two valves—one for letting the mixture into the cylinder during the intake stroke; the other for letting the burned gases pass out into the exhaust manifold after the completion of the firing stroke.

The most common type of valve is the "poppet valve" or mushroom-shaped valve. Its main parts are: head, valve face, and stem. It must be so adjusted that it opens and closes precisely at the proper time, and, when it is shut, it must close perfectly tight. If the "valve face" or the "valve seat" becomes worn, pitted, or warped, the engine will leak gas on the compression and on the firing stroke with a corresponding loss of power. The main causes of loss of compression are piston leak and valve leak. See Fig. 10.

1. Remove a valve from the Ford engine as follows: With a valve-spring compressor raise the valve-spring retainer or washer

and with a pair of pliers remove the valve-seat pin. Place the pin on the table so that it will not be lost. Now pull this valve out through the valve-stem guide. Remove also the valve spring and retainer. Have this work approved by the instructor, then replace the valve, taking care to properly set the valve-seat pin. Make a sketch of a poppet valve, showing valve head, valve face, valve seat, and valve stem. See Dyke.

2. In the operation of a valve state the function of the following parts: the valve spring, the valve lifter, the valve-stem guide, the cam, the cam ears.

3. In a T-head engine how are the valves located with respect to the position of the cylinder?

4. State the position of inlet and exhaust valves during each stroke of a four-stroke engine.

5. In what direction does the engine piston move when the inlet valve is open? When the exhaust valve is open?

6. What is a valve cap and what is its purpose?

7. Distinguish between side valves and overhead valves.

8. Why is it necessary to have clearance between the valve stem and the valve lifter?

9. What amount of clearance is commonly provided?

10. How does heating of the valves and valve stem affect clearance?

11. When clearance is measured what should be the position of the cam?

12. When clearance is measured should the engine be cold or hot?

13. Name two special types of valves other than the common poppet valve.

30. VALVE MECHANISMS—B

Valve Adjustments and Valve Grinding

MATERIALS. Automobile, any standard make; valve push-rod with adjustment screw; valve grinding tools.

A. **Valve Adjustments.** See Dyke. Measure the valve clearance on the laboratory automobile, using two thicknesses of ordinary writing paper as a gauge.

1. Why is it necessary to adjust occasionally the clearance of valves?
2. What is the average lift of the valves of an automobile?
3. If valve clearance is too great how is the operation affected?
4. On many automobiles the valve lifter contains two nuts—the upper one is the head of the adjustment screw and the lower one is a lock nut. Examine these nuts on the automobile. Explain how the adjustment is made. Inquire of the instructor.
5. What trouble sometimes results in using old valve springs?

B. **Valve Grinding and Reseating.** See Dyke.

6. What materials are needed for grinding valves?
7. State the steps in the procedure of preparing to grind valves.
8. How can you determine when a valve is properly ground or when it seats properly?
9. Under what conditions do valves need reseating or reaming?
10. Is loss of compression a certain indication that valves need grinding? Explain.
11. How can you determine whether or not a valve needs grinding?
12. Which valve is more likely to need grinding? Why?
13. What test can be made to determine whether valves leak?

C. **Miscellaneous.**

14. Why is it sometimes necessary to replace valve-stem guides?

15. State procedure in making a test for locating noise due to improper valve adjustment.

16. What troubles may be caused by weak valve springs?

17. Which valves are more likely to become worn—inlet or exhaust? Why?

31. IGNITION INDUCTION COILS

MATERIALS. Vibrating induction coil; make-and-break induction coil; automobile induction coil; wires; five dry cells.

A. **Vibrating Induction Coil.** Connect four dry cells in series and attach one terminal of this dry-cell battery to one of the

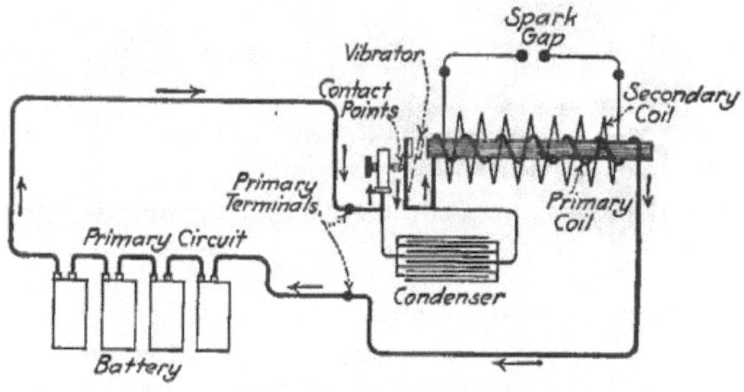

FIG. 33.—Essential parts of a vibrating induction coil.

primary binding posts of the vibrating induction coil. Attach a short wire to one of the secondary binding posts of the induction coil and bend it so that the other end will stand about ¼ inch from the other secondary binding post. (*Caution. Do not operate an induction coil without this wire between the secondary terminals as a protection against short-circuiting when the primary circuit is closed.*)

Now touch the other terminal of the battery to the other primary binding post and notice that hot sparks jump across the spark gap. Note the action of the vibrator. For a description and diagrams of the vibrating induction coil see *Practical Physics*, Millikan, Gale, and Pyle.

1. Compare the two coils of wire with regard to (*a*) number of turns, (*b*) thickness of wire.

2. Diagram the wiring circuits of an induction coil including the vibrator and the condenser. See Millikan, Gale, and Pyle.

3. When a current is passed through the primary coil of the induction coil, what effect is produced upon the soft iron core?

4. Does this effect continue when the current stops flowing?

5. What causes the vibrator to move toward the iron core?

6. What causes the vibrator to move away from the iron core?

7. Where are the contact points of an induction coil located?

8. What important part of the induction coil is connected between the contact points?

9. How does a condenser reduce the spark at the contact points of the vibrator?

10. What effect has this upon the suddenness with which the current is broken in the primary circuit?

11. How does this affect the magnetism surrounding the primary coil?

When a magnetic field is being built up or is being removed from a coil of wire a current of electricity is induced in the coil of wire. The greater the number of turns, the greater the voltage of the induced current. The voltage in the secondary is greater if the change in the magnetic field takes place more quickly.

12. Why is an intermittent current used in the primary of an induction coil?

13. What is the purpose of the adjustment screw at the vibrator?

14. Beginning at the battery trace the primary circuit by naming the parts through which the current passes.

15. What automobile makes use of vibrating induction coils for ignition?

16. How can short-circuiting within the coil be prevented? See *The Gasoline Automobile.*

B. **Simple Make-and-break Induction Coil.** The simple make-and-break induction coil is sometimes used for ignition purposes in

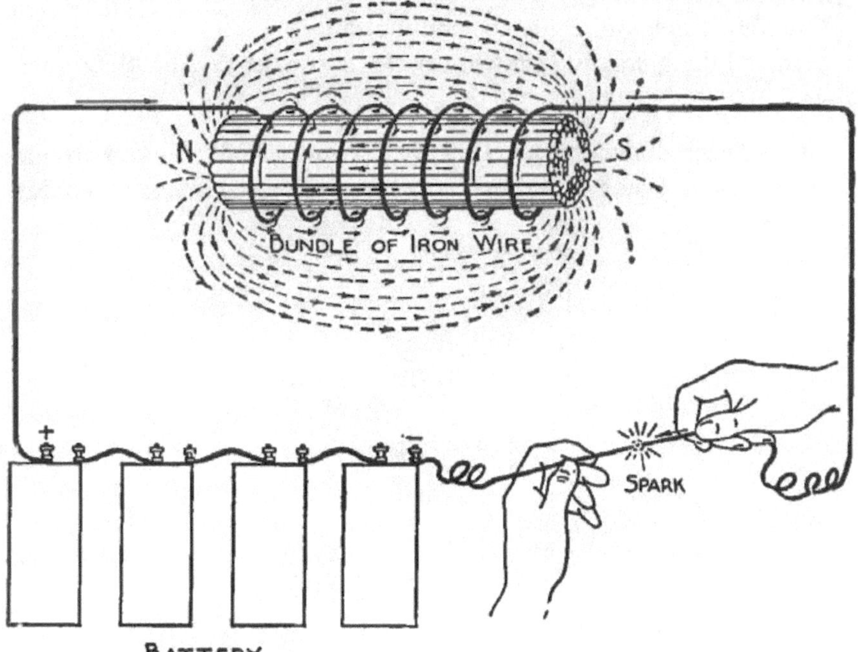

FIG. 34.—Simple make-and-break spark coil sometimes used on gas engines.

small gasoline engines. Connect four dry cells in series. Attach an insulated wire to one terminal of this battery and brush the other end of the wire quickly over the other terminal of the battery. Notice the spark which follows across the gap when the circuit is broken. Attach a wire from one terminal of the battery to one of the primary terminals of the simple make-and-break induction coil. Attach another wire to the other terminal of the coil and brush the free end as before over the other terminal of the battery. Again observe the spark across the gap. This illustrates the use of a simple make-and-break induction coil in an ignition system.

17. Describe the appearance of the make-and-break spark as compared with a jump spark.

18. What causes the high-tension spark when the current in the make-and-break coil is suddenly broken? See *Practical Physics*, Millikan, Gale, and Pyle—Self-induction.

19. Make a diagram showing parts of a make-and-break ignition system?

C. **Automobile Ignition Coil with Timer for Make and Break.** Mount a spark plug on a ring stand. Attach one secondary binding

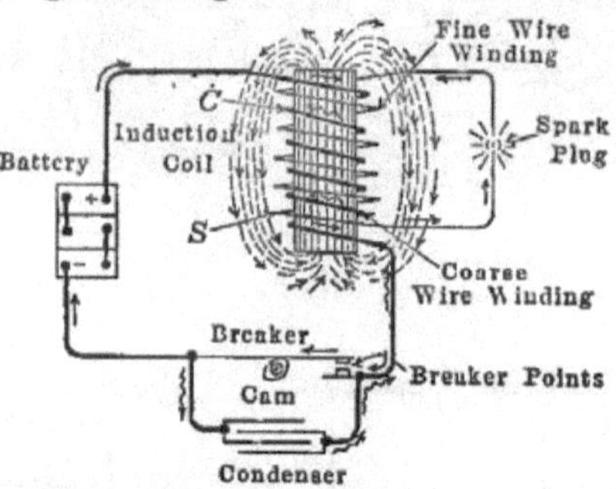

FIG. 35.—Induction coil for jump spark in which the primary circuit is broken by means of a cam as in the timer of an automobile.

post of the automobile coil to the spark plug. Run another wire from the other secondary post to the ring stand to complete the secondary circuit. Attach one terminal of a four-cell battery to one of the primary posts of the coil. Take an insulated wire from the other battery terminal and quickly make and break the primary circuit. Note whether a spark is produced at the spark plug. This kind of induction coil is generally used in automobile ignition systems. On the automobile a device called the timer is used to make and break the primary circuit. A condenser is placed across the contact points of the timer.

20. Make a diagram of an automobile induction coil with timer mechanism including breaker points, contact arm, and condenser shown in the primary circuit. See *The Gasoline Automobile.*

32. IGNITION SYSTEMS—C. STORAGE BATTERY

MATERIALS. Atwater-Kent Ignition unit, Type CC; four dry cells; six spark plugs; ring stands; wires.

A. **Atwater-Kent Ignition System, Type CC.** Read *The Gasoline Automobile* on this ignition system. Study the diagrams and set up the system as follows: Remove the small wire-outlets from the distributor cap and attach seven wires to the distributor binding posts. Connect the center distributor wire to the secondary terminal of the coil. Attach the remaining six wires to six spark plugs mounted on six separate ring stands. Ground the secondary circuit of the coil from the ring stands back to the metal of the ignition unit. Attach one terminal of a battery consisting of four dry cells to the top of the coil and the other terminal to the base of the ignition unit. (Note. In most automobiles a storage battery is used instead of dry cells. Dry cells are used in this experiment merely for convenience.) Turn the timer shaft and see that the spark plugs are firing.

1. What is the source of low-tension current in this system?
2. What is the source of high-tension current in this system?

This form of ignition system is used on most cars that are equipped with storage batteries. The coil is sometimes placed on the instrument board.

B. **The Timer.** Remove the distributor cap and the distributor arm and study the operation of the timer. Note that the condenser is enclosed in the timer housing.

3. Which circuit does the timer make and break?

4. Explain the principle of the condenser. See *Practical Physics*, Millikan, Gale, and Pyle—Induction Coil.

5. What is the function of a condenser connected across the contact points of an induction coil or of a timer in an ignition system? See *Practical Physics*, Millikan, Gale, and Pyle.

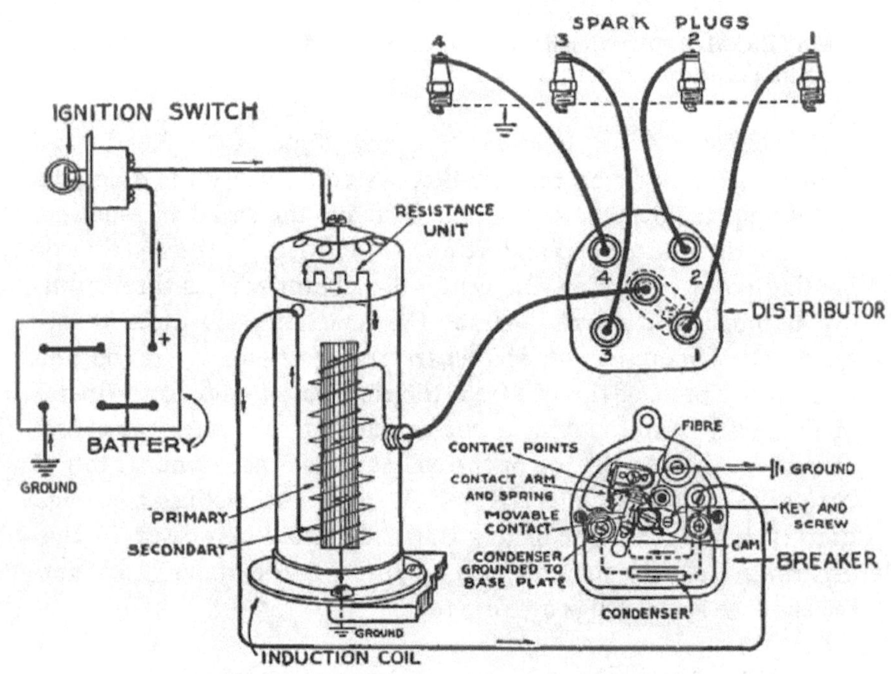

Fig. 36.—Atwater-Kent ignition system, Type CC.

6. Diagram an induction coil with vibrator and condenser.

7. Examine the timer on the car in the laboratory. To what shaft is it attached?

8. State four possible firing orders for six-cylinder engines. Arrange the wiring to give one of these firing orders.

9. What is the shape of the Atwater-Kent timer cam in this

unit? How many times does it make and break the circuit during one revolution?

10. How many times should a six-cylinder engine fire during one revolution of the engine crankshaft? A four-cylinder engine?

11. How many times should this timer revolve while the crankshaft makes one revolution?

12. What would be the shape of the timer in this type of ignition unit for a four-cylinder engine?

13. What provision is made in this mechanism for the advancing and retarding of the spark?

14. Trace the primary circuit in an automobile from the positive battery terminal through the entire ignition circuit and back to the negative terminal, naming the parts of the circuit through which the current passes.

C. **The Distributor.** Replace the distributor arm and study the operation of the distributor.

15. In which circuit is the distributor—primary or secondary?

16. To what shaft is the distributor arm attached?

17. What is the function of the spring located on top of the distributor arm?

18. By naming the parts through which it passes, trace the secondary circuit from the terminal at the side of the coil until it returns to the base of the coil. See diagram, *The Gasoline Automobile.*

19. Make a complete diagram of the Atwater-Kent ignition system. See Fig. 36.

33. IGNITION SYSTEMS—D. FORD CAR

The Ford Ignition System

MATERIALS. Five dry cells; ring stand; spark plugs; Ford engine with coil box mounted on the chassis frame (demonstration car in the laboratory); wires.

The Ford ignition system includes a low-tension magneto generator, a dry-cell battery or storage battery, four induction coils, spark plugs, timer, and ignition switch.

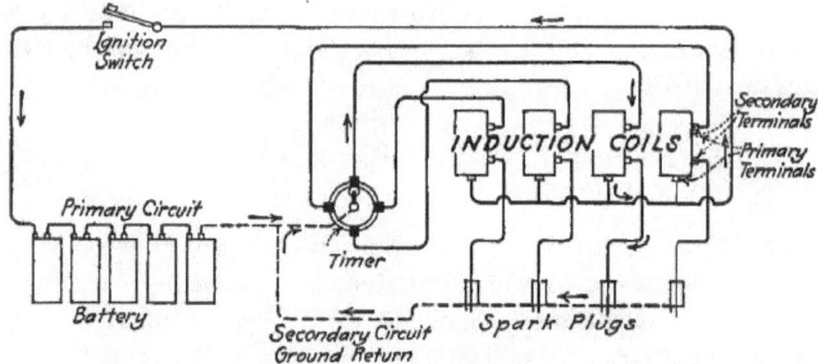

FIG. 37.—The Ford ignition system. Note that the upper terminal of the induction coil serves for both the primary and the secondary circuits.

A. **Ignition Circuits.** Connect five dry cells in series. Attach one terminal of this dry-cell battery to one of the primary binding posts of the induction-coil box (either one of the two lowest posts on the box). Mount a spark plug on a ring stand. Attach one end of a wire to the secondary binding post of one of the induction coils (any one of the middle row of binding posts) and the other end of the wire to the spark plug. Connect a wire from the metal of the ring stand to the metal of the car frame. This completes the secondary circuit. Now attach an insulated wire to the other terminal of the battery and touch this wire to the proper one of the upper row of posts, being very careful not to touch the secondary circuit while the primary circuit is closed. This should produce a spark at the spark plug.

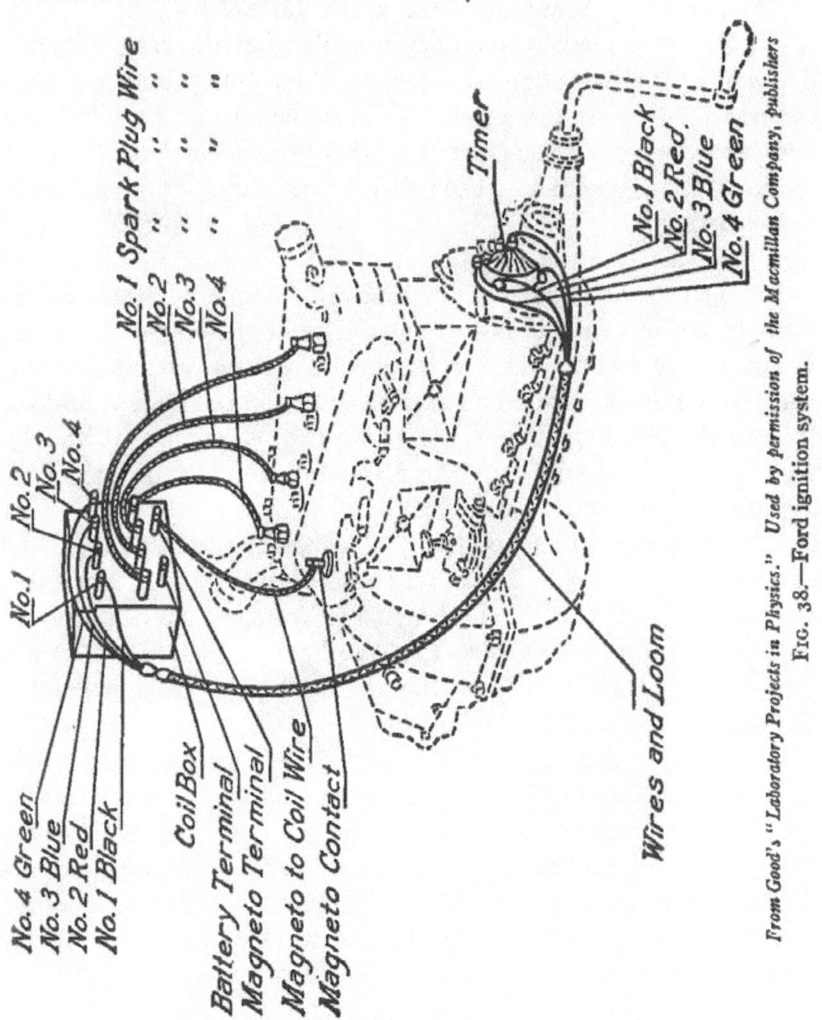

From Good's "Laboratory Projects in Physics." Used by permission of the Macmillan Company, publishers

Fig. 38.—Ford ignition system.

1. Trace the primary circuit in the above arrangement from the positive terminal of the battery back to the negative terminal

of the battery by naming in order the parts through which it passes.

2. Trace the secondary circuit in the same manner, beginning at the secondary terminal of the induction-coil box.

3. Remove one of the induction coils from the case. Make a diagram of the induction coil showing the primary and secondary terminals. One of the three terminals serves for both primary and secondary currents. See *The Gasoline Automobile.*

4. Make a complete wiring diagram of the apparatus used in this experiment.

B. **The Ford Magneto.** The Ford magneto furnishes the primary current for the induction coils after the engine is started. It consists of sixteen small coils of wire wound around soft iron cores which are supported on an iron frame on the engine, and sixteen permanent horseshoe magnets which are attached to the flywheel and revolve with it. The magnets revolving in front of the armature coils induce an alternating current in the coils. The coils are connected in series, one end being connected to the metal of the car (grounded). The other end is connected to the insulated binding post of the flywheel housing from which the current supply is carried to the induction-coil box. The current returns from the induction coils to the magneto coils by a grounded circuit through the frame of the car.

With the spark plug arranged as in *A* of this experiment substitute the magneto for the dry cells by attaching the wire from the magneto binding post to one of the primary binding posts of the induction-coil box. See that the other primary binding post of the coil that you are using is grounded to the frame of the car. Use the crank to revolve the flywheel as rapidly as you can. Sparks should be produced at the spark plug.

5. Turn the crank at different speeds and state whether low or high speed gives the better spark. Why?

6. Why is a Ford car usually hard to start by cranking if the magneto current is used for ignition when starting?

C. **The Ford Ignition System.** Attach both battery and magneto to the induction coils as in *A* and *B* of this experiment. Attach four wires from the four upper primary binding posts of the coil box to the four posts of the timer cap on the front of the engine. Do not permit the ends of the wires at the timer posts to touch the metal of the engine or the metal body of the timer cap. Attach wires from the four secondary binding posts of the coil box to the four spark plugs on the engine. Turn the ignition switch so that the battery supplies the current for ignition and touch each post of the timer in turn with the wire from the battery and notice that the spark plugs fire. Turn the switch so that the magneto supplies the current for ignition and with the crank revolve the flywheel and notice that the four spark plugs are firing. The firing order of the Ford, beginning with the front cylinder as No. 1, should be 1, 2, 4, 3. If your firing order is not correct, arrange the wires from the coil to the timer so that the firing order will be correct. Remove the timer cap and examine the action of the timer roller when the crank is turned. Now attach the wire from the battery to any part of the metal of the engine or frame. If the ignition switch is in the proper position the plugs should spark in the proper sequence when the engine is cranked.

7. What is the purpose of the timer? What is the function of the roller in the timer?

8. With respect to the speed of the crankshaft at what rate does the timer arm revolve?

9. To what shaft is the timer attached? What causes this shaft to revolve?

10. What other function does this shaft perform?

11. Locate the four inlet valves by observing the two openings into which the intake manifold leads. By turning the crank

determine in what order the inlet valves open beginning with the front cylinder as No. 1. State this order.

12. How should the firing order compare with the order in which the inlet valves open? If the firing order of an engine is not known how can it readily be determined?

13. What is the function of the ignition switch? Why should it always be turned off when the car is not running?

14. When should the battery be used on a Ford car?

15. Is the timer of the Ford placed in the primary or the secondary circuit of the coils?

D. **Ignition Troubles.** Reference: Dyke. See also *Ford Supplement.*

16. Give four possible causes for the spark plugs missing fire.

17. Tell how you could locate a missing cylinder.

18. How could you test a spark plug?

19. Tell how you could determine whether or not the battery is weak.

34. IGNITION SYSTEMS—E. LOW-TENSION MAGNETO AND DRY-CELL BATTERY

MATERIALS. Low-tension magneto generator and induction coil; ignition switch; timer (attached to magneto); distributor (attached to magneto); ring stands; spark plugs; wires; five dry cells.

A. **Remy, Model RL, Ignition System.** Read *The Gasoline Automobile* on this system. After studying the diagram attach the induction coil to the magneto. Connect the five dry cells to the primary circuit of the coil. Mount four spark plugs on four separate ring stands. Attach the center distributor wire to the secondary circuit of the coil and the remaining four distributor wires to the four spark plugs. Ground the secondary circuit from the ring stands back to the metal of the ignition switch and coil.

Attach the three wires from the magneto to the proper binding posts of the coil. Operate the system by revolving the armature

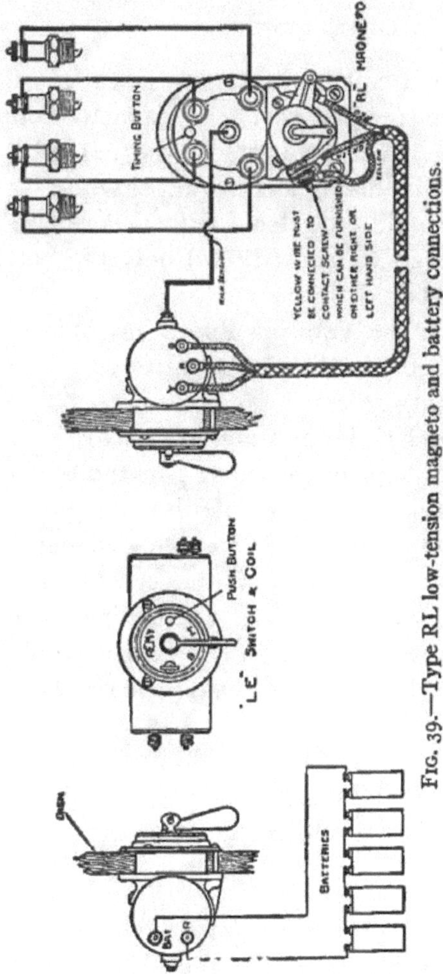

Fig. 39.—Type RL low-tension magneto and battery connections.

shaft of the magneto (by hand) with the switch on magneto (*M*) and then on battery (*B*) and see that it works in both cases. See Fig. 73.

1. State one advantage and one disadvantage of this kind of ignition system.

2. Why must dry cells be used in this system?

3. Explain how the magneto is connected to the automobile.

B. **Timer and Distributor.**

4. In which circuit of the coil is the timer? the distributor?

5. Will either the battery or the magneto produce a spark if the yellow cord (*Y*) is disconnected? the red cord (*R*)? the green cord (*G*)? Test by disconnecting proper wires.

6. Where would you look first for a disconnected cord if (*a*) only the magneto worked? (*b*) only the battery? (*c*) neither magneto nor battery?

7. What are the two possible firing orders of four-cylinder engines? Connect the distributor wires to the proper spark plugs to give these firing orders.

8. To what shaft is the timer attached?

9. Note the shape of the timer cam and tell how many times it makes and breaks the primary circuit in one revolution.

10. How many times does a single-cylinder four-stroke engine fire during one revolution of the crankshaft? a two-cylinder engine? a four-cylinder engine? a six-cylinder engine?

11. How many times should this timer revolve while the crankshaft of a four-cylinder engine makes one revolution? a six-cylinder engine?

12. Carefully take off the distributor cap by removing the two large screws at the sides and explain how the distributor is operated. After observing this mechanism replace the distributor cap and the screws.

A low-tension alternating-current magneto of this type is sometimes used on trucks which are not provided with a storage battery. The engine must be cranked by hand. Most automobiles having storage batteries use the storage battery for ignition current on starting.

35. IGNITION SYSTEMS—F. HIGH-TENSION MAGNETOS

MATERIALS. One or more high-tension magnetos such as the Bosch, type DU4; the Eisemann, type G4; the Berling, type F41; the Dixie (inductor type) or the K–W (inductor type); reference books and instruction books.

Caution. Do not operate this magneto while you are or anyone else is touching the secondary circuit, as a severe shock may result.

Connect the terminals of the distributor with four spark plugs which have been mounted in ring stands as in the preceding ignition experiments. Connect a ground wire from the ring stands back to the metal of the magneto to complete the high-tension circuit. Operate the magneto and see that each plug sparks at the proper time.

A. **Magnetos.**

1. How does a " hot spark " differ in appearance from a " lean spark " ? Does a magneto ignition system give as hot a spark at low speed as at high speed? Why?

2. Should spark-plug gaps be as wide for magneto ignition as for battery ignition? What is the approximate width of gap for magnetos? See *Motor Vehicles.*

3. What does the usual type of high-tension magneto armature have which the low-tension magneto does not have?

4. Make a simple diagram representing the wiring of a high-tension magneto. See *The Gasoline Automobile* or *Motor Vehicles.* Place pencil arrows on the low-tension circuit and ink arrows on the high-tension circuit.

5. What effect must occur at the interrupter to produce the high-tension current in the secondary circuit?

6. In approximately what position does the armature core stand when this occurs?

7. What magnetic effect is being produced in the armature at this time?

8. In which circuit is the switch placed? What is its function?

9. Why does a magneto interrupter cam usually make two breaks of the contact points per revolution instead of one?

B. **The Bosch Magneto.**

10. Describe the location of (*a*) the primary coil, (*b*) the secondary coil, (*c*) condenser, (*d*) the interrupter, (*e*) the distributor.

11. Explain how the high-tension current is carried from the secondary coil to the distributor arm.

12. Through how many degrees does the spark advance lever move?

13. By what kind of bearings is the armature supported?

14. State the special features of the Bosch High-tension Dual System. See *The Gasoline Automobile.*

C. **The Dixie Magneto.** See *The Gasoline Automobile.*

15. Where are the coils located in this magneto?

16. Do these coils move or are they stationary?

17. Has the rotor of this type of magneto any wire on it? Of what material is it made? What is the function of the bronze center?

18. With respect to the operation of the coils of this magneto what is the specific function of the rotor as it revolves?

D. **Troubles.**

19. State at least four possible magneto troubles. See *The Gasoline Automobile.*

36. STORAGE BATTERY—B

MATERIALS. Storage battery (commercial type preferably in glass jar); battery hydrometer; battery ammeter; rheostat.

Caution. Sulphuric acid will destroy clothing and cause burns. Handle with extreme care.

A. **Operation.** Examine the large storage batteries. Test by means of a salt solution, as in Storage Battery—A, to find which

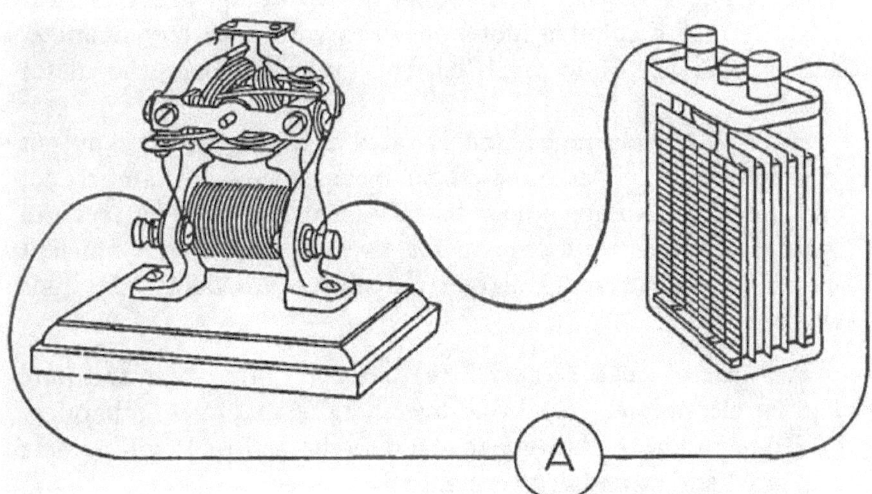

From Good's "Laboratory Projects in Physics." Used by permission of the Macmillan Company, publishers

FIG. 40.—A storage battery operating a motor with an ammeter in the circuit.

terminal is negative. Test the line current also to find which terminal is negative. With a 3-ampere rheostat in series, prepare to force a current through the battery in reverse direction (positive connected to positive and negative to negative). (*Caution. Have your scheme of wiring inspected by an instructor before turning on the current, to avoid a possibility of ruining the batteries.*) If necessary, distilled water should be added so that the electrolyte stands $\frac{1}{4}$ inch above the plates. The time required for complete charge from condition of discharge is usually fifteen to twenty hours.

1. Do not attach an ammeter to a storage battery without additional resistance in the circuit. Why?
2. Record the specific gravity at the beginning of charge.
3. Charge for fifteen minutes. This brief time will not make a measurable change on the specific gravity. Does the acid become more or less concentrated on charging? Refer to texts.
4. What is the combined voltage of two storage cells in series?
5. Attach a suitable motor in series with a battery ammeter and operate it. How much current (amperes) does the motor take?

Storage batteries are commonly rated as having a certain output in ampere-hours. An ampere-hour means a flow of 1 ampere for one hour. A 20-ampere-hour battery means that the battery can supply a current of 1 ampere for twenty hours, after which it should be recharged. If larger amperages are taken, the time will be reduced.

B. **Care of Lead Battery.** (*a*) Use only pure water and pure acid for electrolyte. (*b*) Avoid overcharging and overdischarging. (*c*) Do not allow the battery to stand discharged, as it will become sulphated and sometimes permanently injured.

In the self-starting systems of automobiles, storage batteries are required to deliver between 50 and 200 amperes at about 6 volts for a few moments in starting the engine. This large amperage would soon exhaust and injure a storage battery. The starting motor should be operated for very short periods only. Lead storage batteries are well suited for this work, because they can deliver an enormous current for a short time, due to their very low internal resistance. Automobile storage batteries have a specific gravity at complete charge 1.3, and at complete discharge 1.15.

C. **Reference Work.** *The Gasoline Automobile.*

6. What is meant by (*a*) grid, (*b*) separator, (*c*) negative terminal, (*d*) specific gravity?

7. What two forms of lead are used in the making of plates?

8. How does the formation of insoluble lead sulphate reduce the efficiency of the cell?

9. What is meant by the expression, 10-ampere, eight-hour cell?

10. For what length of time should a cell rated at 100 ampere-hours produce a current of 5 amperes?

11. If cells are discharged too rapidly, what tends to reduce their efficiency?

37. STORAGE BATTERY—C

Construction, Operation, Tests, and Troubles

MATERIALS. Automobile batteries, if possible, one in section; syringe type of hydrometer in a large bottle; reference books.

The lead storage battery requires exceptional care. Its construction and principles should be thoroughly studied by every automobile owner. Of all the automobile equipment there is no more delicate piece of apparatus, and yet, the storage battery, due chiefly to ignorance, is one of the most neglected and abused units of the car. To replace a worn-out battery involves a considerable expense that could often be avoided by a few hours of study and attention to a few simple testing operations. Read *The Gasoline Automobile* and *Motor Vehicles*.

1. What proportions of distilled water and sulphuric acid should be used in making up a lead storage battery electrolyte?

2. In the ordinary operation of a car, about how frequently should the storage battery be refilled with distilled water?

3. What evidence that a battery is being overcharged may be observed in the action of the electrolyte?

4. What injurious effect is caused by undercharging a battery?

5. What is the highest temperature which a storage battery should be permitted to reach?

6. What is the normal temperature for taking hydrometer readings of a storage battery?

7. At what temperature will a battery freeze—(*a*) if it is fully charged? (*b*) if it is completely discharged?

8. Under what conditions might a motor-generator be used in charging a storage battery?

9. Why is it necessary to use a resistance in the circuit in charging a battery with 110-volt current?

10. Make a diagram showing apparatus needed for charging a battery. Indicate the name of each part, including the positive and the negative terminals of the battery and of the supply line.

11. Explain the meaning of *charge rate* and *finish rate* in charging a battery.

12. State the method of determining when a battery is fully charged with respect to (*a*) change in voltage and in specific gravity, (*b*) the voltage with charging current on, (*c*) gassing, (*d*) specific gravity.

13. If, after continuous charging, a battery does not show a sufficiently high specific gravity, what is probably needed?

14. What are the causes of sulphation? How may sulphation be prevented?

15. Is sulphate a conductor of electricity? How does this affect the charging of a sulphated battery?

16. How may a sulphated battery be partly restored?

17. When a battery is filled, how high should the level of the liquid stand above the plates? If it is filled too full, what trouble occurs when the battery is being charged?

18. What causes battery plates to buckle or warp?

19. How could one of the cells of a battery be tested to find out whether it is "dead"?

20. Name ten common causes which tend to overdischarge and injure a storage battery.

38. OPERATING A GAS ENGINE—TROUBLES AND ADJUSTMENTS

Study of a Gas Engine in Operation

MATERIALS. One and one-half horsepower gasoline engine on truck.

Operate the engine with illuminating gas (or with gasoline) and study its operation and adjustments.

1. What kind of mixture causes a gas or gasoline engine to "back fire" into the intake manifold and carburetor?

2. Devise a scheme for causing this engine to "back fire." (Note. If you are in doubt about any procedure in this experiment, consult with the instructor before using it.)

3. Hold your thumb over the air intake and note the effect upon the operation of the engine. How could an automobile driver cause a trouble similar to this while driving?

4. How could you cause trouble in this engine similar to that which occurs when a carburetor spray needle is too far shut? Try it.

5. How could you cause trouble in this engine similar to that which occurs when an exhaust valve leaks? What effect is produced?

6. How could you cause this engine to explode in the muffler as in the case of a leaky exhaust valve? Try it.

7. How could you cause trouble in this engine similar to that which occurs when an inlet valve leaks? Try it.

8. Is it possible to make this engine "kick back" (revolve in the reverse direction)? Explain.

9. Does the spark in this engine occur at "top center" of the compression stroke or before "top center"? Give a reason for your answer.

10. Is there any provision on this engine for timing the ignition? What is it?

11. What provision is made for timing the exhaust valve?

12. How could you demonstrate on this engine the effect of weak valve springs? Try it.

13. Name at least six possible places in the combustion chamber of this engine which might be out of adjustment and cause leakage.

14. Name at least five ignition troubles which might occur on this engine. Consult *The Gasoline Automobile.*

39. ENGINE TROUBLES

Reference Work, *The Gasoline Automobile.*

A. **Classification of Engine Troubles.**

1. Name eleven main groups of symptoms under which engine troubles are classified.

2. Which of these symptoms may result from carburetor troubles?

3. Which of these symptoms may result from ignition troubles?

4. State symptoms which may result from spark-plug troubles.

5. State symptoms which may result from compression leakage.

6. State symptoms which may result from valve troubles.

7. State symptoms which may result from improper lubrication.

8. State seven possible troubles if an engine knocks.

9. What are the possible troubles if an engine misses at low speeds?

10. Of what use is such a table of symptoms and troubles to an intelligent repairman?

B. **Engine Trouble Chart,** *The Gasoline Automobile.*

11. What carburetor troubles are mentioned?

12. What troubles are represented as pertaining to valves and valve mechanisms?

13. State troubles pertaining to crankshafts, connecting rods, and pistons.

14. State troubles pertaining to (*a*) the cooling system; (*b*) the ignition system.

40. CHANGE-SPEED GEARS—A. SELECTIVE

MATERIALS. Automobile chassis and reference books.

Practice shifting the gears to obtain the different speeds. Turn the engine over by means of the crank. Open the cylinder pet cocks.

1. Make a diagram showing the position for low, intermediate, high, and reverse gears. See *The Gasoline Automobile.*

2. What are the two common types of gear-shift levers?

3. What is the location of the gear case in the laboratory automobile? What two other locations are sometimes used? What are the advantages and disadvantages of each type? See *Motor Vehicles.*

4. What are the common types of gear transmission? What are the advantages of the selective type? See *Motor Vehicles.*

Transmission gear ratio means the rate of engine or crankshaft speed compared with the rear axle or rear wheel speed.

5. By counting the teeth determine the gear ratio of the drive shaft pinion (in the differential housing) and the differential ring gear. This is the gear ratio between the driveshaft and the rear-axle shaft.

6. Determine the gear ratio between the crankshaft and the propeller shaft when the transmission is in high, low, intermediate, and reverse gears. To do this put chalk marks on the propeller shaft and flywheel, then turn the motor by hand and count the number of revolutions of the motor to one revolution of the propeller shaft. This should be checked up later by counting the proper gear teeth in the gear case.

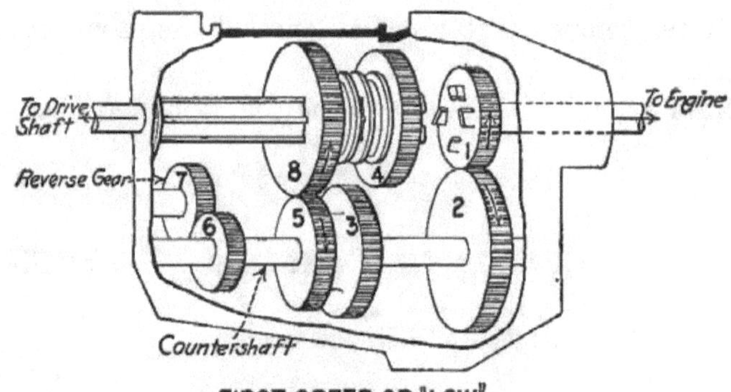

FIG. 41*a*.—Position of gears in three speed and reverse gear set. First or "low" speed position.

7. State the gear ratio between the crankshaft and the rear axle for high, intermediate, and low gears.

8. In which gear will the car have the greatest pull—high, intermediate, low, or reverse? Explain.

Remove the gear-case cover.

9. What two shafts are found within the gear box? See *Motor Vehicles* and *The Gasoline Automobile*.

10. How many gears are on each shaft?

11. Which shaft is in constant motion when the main driving gear is in motion? See Dyke, Transmission.

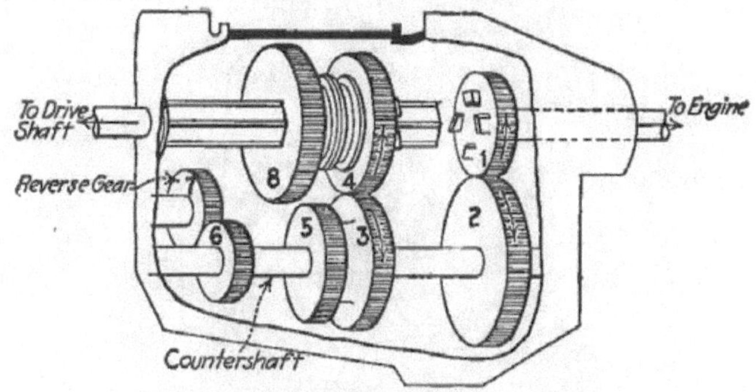

FIG. 41*b*.—Position of gears in three speed and reverse gear set. Second or "intermediate" speed position.

12. Which shaft has gears that slide back and forward? How many sliding gears does it have?

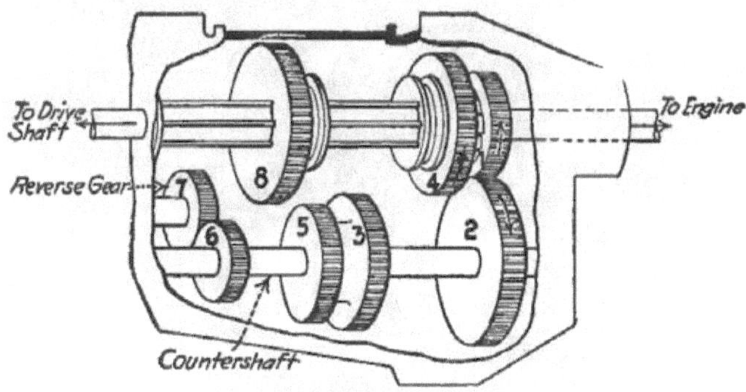

FIG. 41*c*.—Position of gears in three speed and reverse gear set. Third or "high" speed position.

13. What is the function of these sliding gears?

14. Which speeds does the front sliding gear control?

15. Which speeds does the rear sliding gear control?
16. How does the reverse gear system work?

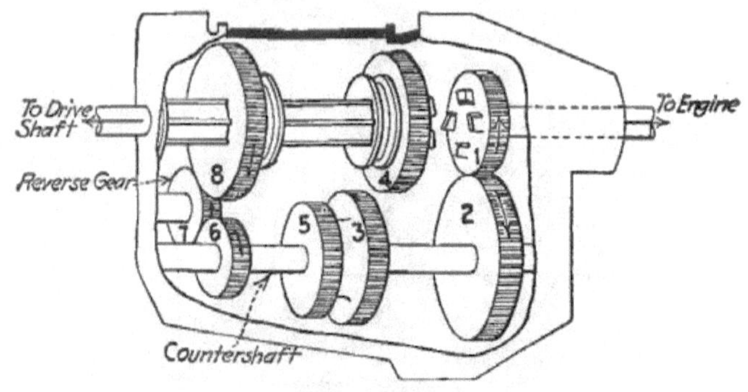

FIG. 41*d*.—Position of gears in three speed and reverse gear set. Reverse speed position.

17. What are the dogs on the front sliding gear, and what is their purpose? See *Motor Vehicles*.

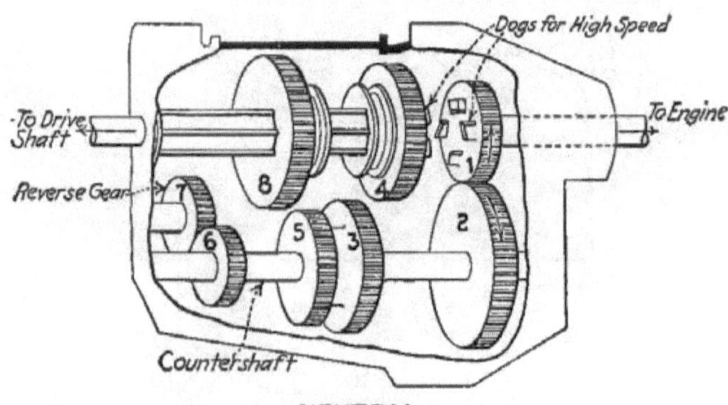

FIG. 41*e*.—Position of gears in three speed and reverse gear set. Neutral Position.

18. Make a diagram showing a selective type of transmission with the gears in neutral.

41. CHANGE-SPEED GEARS—B. FORD TRANSMISSION.

The Planetary Gears and the Clutch

MATERIALS. Ford chassis and reference books.

Operate the gears of the Ford car in the following manner: By means of a suitable bolt compress one of the brake bands so that it grips the middle one of the three drums. This causes the planetary gear mechanism to operate the drive shaft in "low gear." (The drive shaft goes slower than the crankshaft or engine.)

1. Place a chalk mark on the clutch housing or brake drum. Let one person crank the engine over eleven turns while the other counts the number of revolutions made by the clutch housing and consequently the drive shaft. What is the gear ratio of low gear between the crankshaft and the driveshaft on the Ford car?

2. In the operation of a set of gears the pull is increased in the same ratio as the speed is decreased (friction not being considered). If we do not consider waste power due to friction how much greater should a Ford car be able to pull when it is in "low" than when it is in "high"? Does friction make the actual force or push of the rear wheels greater or less than this amount?

3. Move the brake band to the drum nearest the flywheel. Crank the engine as before. When this drum is prevented from revolving, what effect is produced upon the direction of motion of the clutch housing and consequently of the drive shaft?

4. In the same manner as before determine the gear ratio when the gears are operating in reverse.

5. On the basis of the reverse gear ratio how much greater should the Ford car be able to push than to pull in high (friction not being considered)?

6. If a Ford car is unable to go up a steep hill in low gear, it is sometimes possible to back the car up the hill. Explain.

7. What is the purpose of the third brake drum—the one farthest from the flywheel?

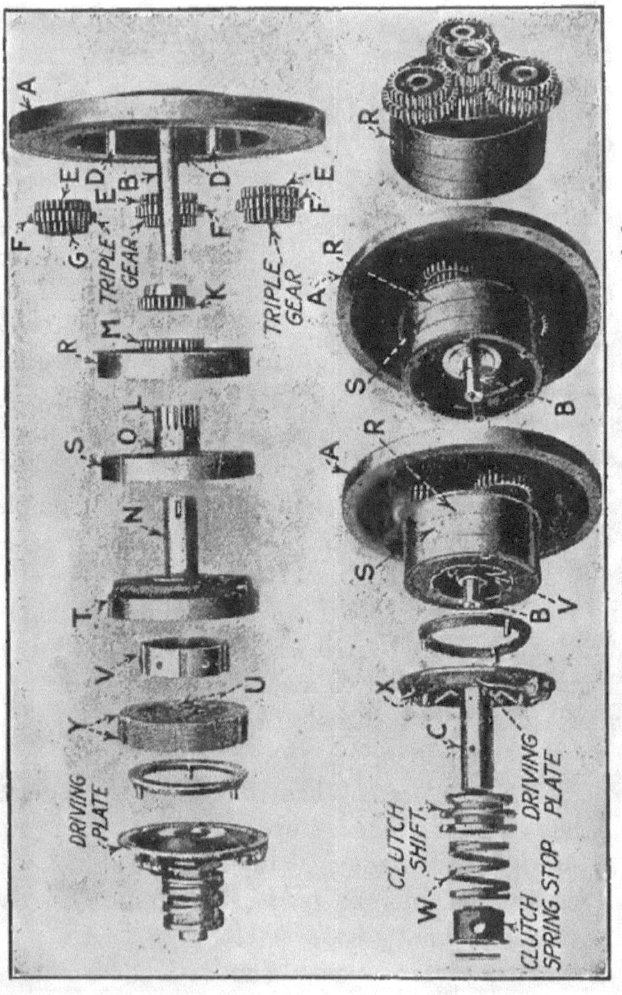

FIG. 42.—Disassembled view of Ford planetary transmission.

B. **The Ford Clutch.** *Multiple Disc*, Dyke.

8. Where is the clutch located in the Ford transmission? See *Motor Vehicles* and Dyke's *Ford Supplement.*

9. Note that a shaft called the transmission shaft extends from the flywheel through the gear mechanism into the clutch housing. This shaft is connected to the flywheel and therefore must run with the crankshaft and at the same speed as the crankshaft. Which of the clutch plates or discs are attached to the end of the transmission shaft? How many of these discs are used?

10. To what part of the transmission assembly are the large clutch discs attached? How many of these are used?

11. When the engine is running in high gear how is the connection made between the transmission shaft and the drive shaft?

12. What parts of the mechanism keep the clutch engaged?

13. In operation of the car what two levers compress the clutch spring and disengage the clutch?

42. CHANGE-SPEED GEARS—C. FORD TRANSMISSION

The Planetary Gears and the Clutch

MATERIALS. Ford chassis; reference books and the *Ford Manual*.

A. **The Ford Gears.** This type of gear mechanism has been called planetary on account of a fanciful resemblance to the planets revolving around the sun in the solar system. The Ford transmission provides for high, low, and reverse. High speed is obtained by a direct connection with the clutch by means of the "transmission shaft." See Dyke. The gear mechanism provides for low speed and reverse. With a suitable bolt compress the brake bands and observe the operation of the gear mechanism.

1. How many sets of triple gears are provided on the Ford? Note that these triple gears are set on shafts which are fastened to the flywheel. The triple-gear shafts must therefore move when the crankshaft and the flywheel move. Note that the three wheels which constitute each triple gear are all fastened together

into a single unit. They all move together at the same rate and in the same direction.

2. Release the brake bands from the low and the reverse drums and crank the engine in high gear. In high gear do the triple gears revolve on their shafts?

3. When do the triple gears sets revolve on their shafts?

4. Do they revolve on their shafts in the same direction in both "low" and "reverse"?

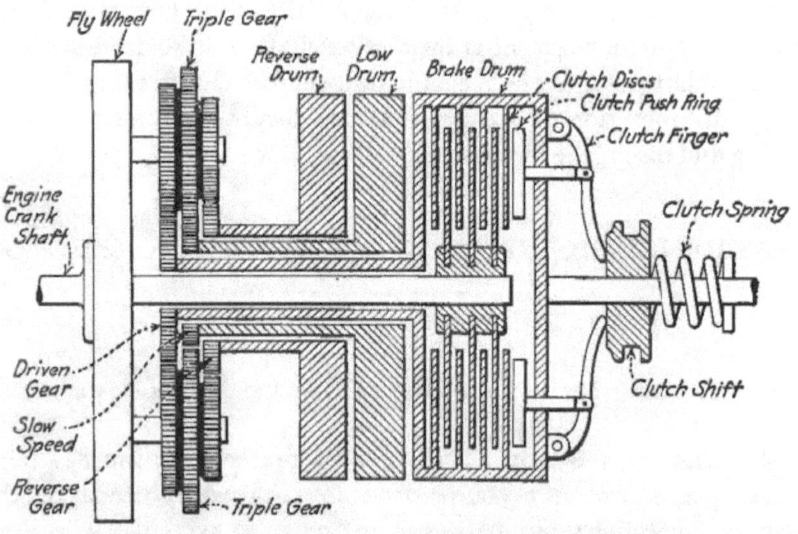

FIG. 43.—Diagram showing the principle of the Ford transmission.

5. How many center gears ("sun gears") are provided? Note that each gear of a triple-gear set engages with a center gear. One center gear connects with the clutch housing; one connects with the low-speed drum; and one connects with the reverse drum.

6. Which one of the triple gears is the largest? Which is the smallest?

7. Which of the center gears (sun gears) is the largest? Which is the smallest?

8. Are the three center gears fastened together like the triple-gear sets or do they move separately?

9. Which of the three center gears is connected with the clutch housing and therefore may move with the propeller shaft?

10. Which of the three center gears is connected with the low-gear drum? Which with the reverse drum? How can you show this definitely by experiment?

11. Place a brake band on the low-gear drum and bolt it, holding the drum still. Which of the three center gears is held still?

12. When the engine is now cranked do the triple gears revolve clockwise or counterclockwise (looking at them from the rear of the car)?

13. What causes the triple gears to revolve in this case?

14. In which direction does this cause the center gear nearest the flywheel to revolve (clockwise or counterclockwise)? Note that this gear is attached to the clutch housing and to the drive shaft. Does this gear revolve at the same rate as the flywheel? What is its ratio?

15. Now clamp the brake band on the reverse drum and crank the engine. Which of the center gears is held stationary?

16. Do the triple gears revolve clockwise or counterclockwise? Note that they revolve faster than in the case of low gear.

17. In which direction does this cause the center gear which controls the drive shaft to revolve?

B. **The Clutch.** The Ford clutch can be engaged only in high gear. In low and reverse it must be released.

18. Explain why the clutch must be released when the gears are in low or reverse.

19. What disengages the clutch when low gear is used?

20. What disengages the clutch when reverse is used?

43. CLUTCHES

The Multiple Disc Clutch and the Cone Clutch

MATERIALS. The Ford chassis; the *Ford Manual* and reference books.

A. **The Multiple Disc Clutch—Disassembling the Ford Clutch.** See Fig. 42. Raise the rear end of the motor and support it so that the clutch will be accessible. This may be done by removing the bolts between the engine block and the crankcase. Then raise

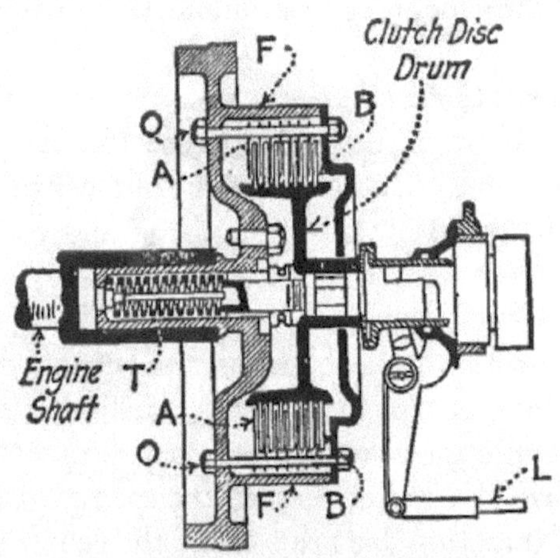

FIG. 44.—A multiple-disc clutch.

the rear end of the engine and place a board under the transmission drums. Follow the directions in the *Ford Manual* for disassembling the clutch mechanism. Remove the driving plate, then remove the push ring.

NOTE. Place all bolts and parts carefully and orderly on a newspaper to avoid losing them and to aid in reassembling. Then remove the clutch discs. When the clutch is completely disassembled, have the work inspected by the instructor. For reference, use the *Ford Manual* and *Motor Vehicles.*

1. How many discs does the Ford have?
2. What is the purpose of the large discs? of the small discs?

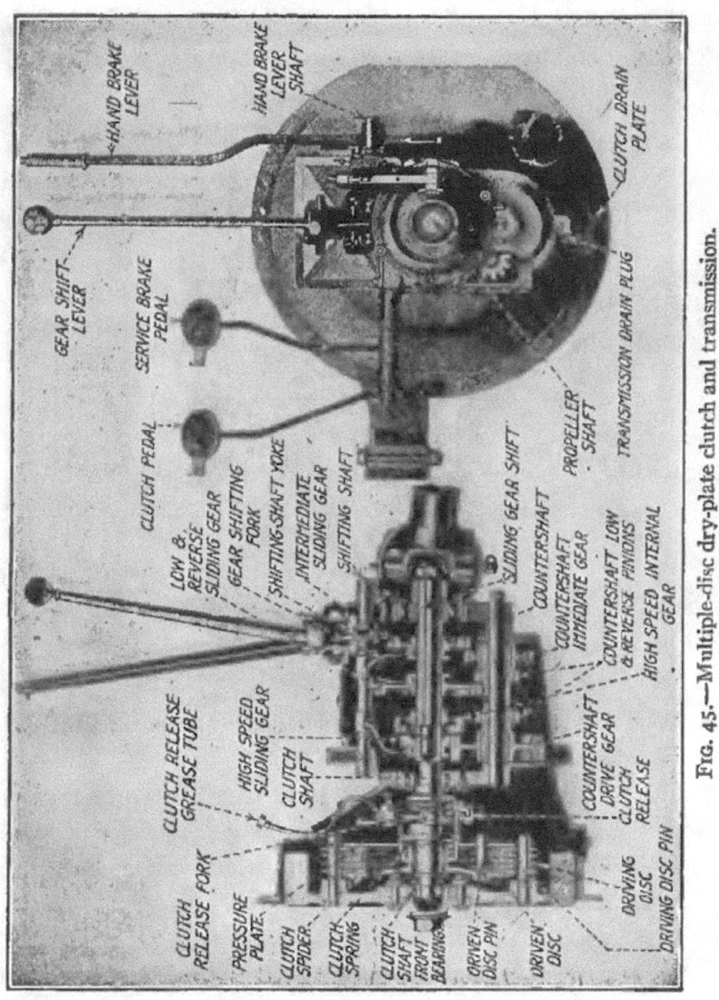

Fig. 45.—Multiple-disc dry-plate clutch and transmission.

3. To what are the large discs connected? How is this connection made?

4. To what are the small discs connected? How is this connection made?

5. Of what material are the discs made?

Reassemble the clutch and have your work inspected and approved by the instructor. Do not continue further until this is done.

6. What is the purpose of the clutch?

7. Describe the relative positions of the large and small discs when the clutch is engaged and when disengaged.

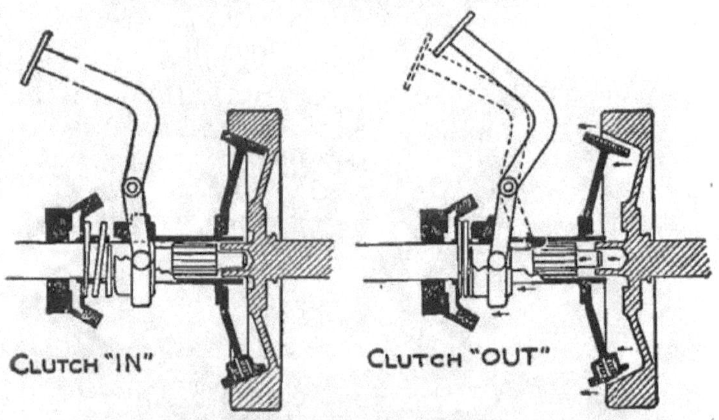

FIG. 46.—Cone clutch showing "in" and "out" positions.

8. What releases the plates? What engages the plates?

9. How are the discs held in contact?

10. What would be the result if the discs did not engage closely or firmly? How may this defect be remedied?

11. Does the clutch need to be lubricated? If so, what means are provided for lubrication?

12. In the operation of the clutch mechanism state the purpose of: (*a*) the discs; (*b*) the clutch release plate; (*c*) the clutch fork; (*d*) the spring; (*e*) the clutch shift; (*f*) the clutch finger.

13. Explain how the emergency-brake lever releases the clutch. Why is it necessary to do this?

14. What is the position of the clutch when the Ford car is running (*a*) in low gear; (*b*) in reverse gear; (*c*) in high gear? Is it the same in the case of other cars?

B. **The Cone Clutch.** Read *The Gasoline Automobile* on the cone clutch. If possible, examine a cone clutch.

FIG. 47.—A typical cone clutch.

15. What are the two most common types of clutches?

16. Why is this mechanism called a cone clutch? How many degrees, approximately, does it taper?

17. What materials are used in facing cone clutches?

18. What holds a clutch engaged and what releases it?

19. Do cone clutches operate dry or in oil?

20. Make a simple diagram of a cone clutch mechanism with parts labeled.

44. BRAKE MECHANISMS—B

Brakes Used on the Larger Cars

MATERIALS. Automobile chassis; reference books.

Brakes which do not operate properly when an emergency arises are responsible for a large proportion of automobile accidents.

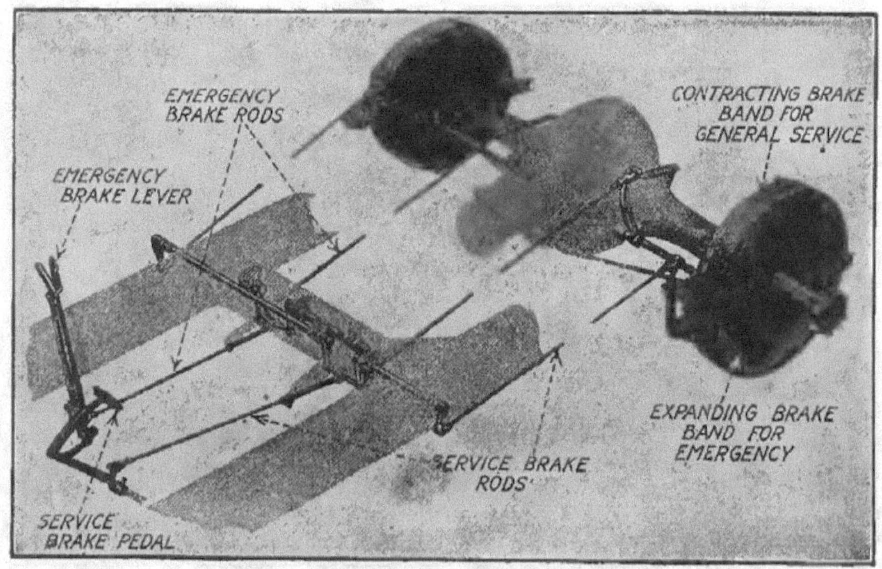

Fig. 48.—Braking system on Cadillac eight.

Brakes that are too tight will cause loss of power and unnecessary wear on the friction surfaces. Examine the illustrations of brake mechanism in the reference books.

Remove the hub cap and the lock nut from one of the rear wheels of the large laboratory automobile. Take off the wheel. For this work get directions from the instructor. Place all nuts, screws, and small parts on a table to avoid losing them. As a reference book for this work use Dyke.

1. What prevents the lock nut from coming off when the car is in operation?

2. Examine the brake mechanism. Name the two general classes of brake mechanisms. In this car which of the two is used for service brake and which for the emergency brake?

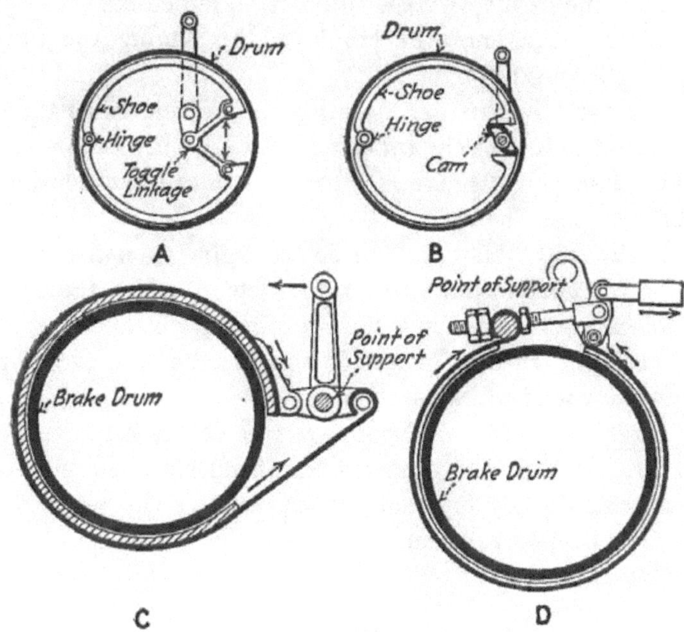

FIG. 49.—Types of expanding and contracting brakes.

3. State the function of the following parts of a brake mechanism: brake band lever, release spring, cam, or toggle mechanism.

4. With what material are brake bands commonly lined?

5. What are the characteristics of an ideal brake lining?

6. In this braking system how many brake-rods or cables extend between the brakeshaft and the brakes?

7. When the driver applies the brakes by what means is the force carried to the brakeshafts?

Replace the wheel on the hub with key and lock nut in proper position. Have the work approved by the instructor before putting on the hub cap.

Troubles and Adjustments.

8. What are four troubles usually experienced with brakes? See texts.

9. Explain the cause of each of these troubles.

10. How may each of these troubles be remedied?

11. What means may be employed for saving the brakes in descending a long hill?

12. If a car tends to skid or swing to one side when the brakes are set, what defect in the brake adjustment may be the cause?

13. Explain how a brake equalizer provides equal tension upon both brakes. See Dyke.

14. If the brake band should be too tight when the brakes are in the "off" position locate the stop screw by which the band may be set looser. A band should show a clearance of about $\frac{1}{16}$ inch all the way around when released. It should take hold evenly all the way around when brakes are applied.

15. Have the external brake rods or cables inspected by the instructor. If they are properly equalized set them so that the external brakes apply unequally, then equalize them. If they are unequally set equalize them. State your procedure.

45. COMPRESSION—A

Simple Tests of Compression

MATERIALS. Laboratory automobile engine and reference books.

In the operation of the engine the intake stroke of the piston carries the mixture into the cylinder. Then the intake valve closes and, as the piston comes up on the compression stroke, the charge is compressed in the upper end of the cylinder. At the end of the compression stroke the firing or power stroke occurs and the piston is forced downward by the explosion. If, for any reason, leaks occur around the pistons, valves, or other points in the combustion chamber, the engine will waste gasoline and consequently lose power. Compression losses become very large in the case of old or abused engines.

A. **Compression.** The piston is at top center on the compression stroke approximately one revolution after the intake valve begins to open. Make a simple compression test as follows: Open the throttle completely and turn off the ignition switch. Open all compression or priming cocks except the one on the cylinder which you wish to test. Note when the intake valve for that cylinder opens. Turn slowly one revolution further, noting the effect as compression is passed.

1. Describe the condition of the compression in the case of each of the four cylinders, beginning with the front as No. 1. If it turns through compression easily write "poor compression." If it passes compression with difficulty and with springy resistance write "good compression."
2. Name six different kinds of compression leaks. See *Motor Vehicles*.
3. How may leaks past gaskets, valve caps, spark plugs, priming cocks, etc., be detected?
4. If none of the leaks mentioned in question 3 exist, how can you next test for piston leak?
5. Name two other possible causes of compression leakage.
6. Name three possible causes of valve leakage.

B. **Compression Test.** Test the compression of the laboratory automobile engine as follows: Proceed as above and stop the piston at top center on the compression stroke. This may require some practice to avoid letting the piston slip past top center. Let your associate hold a watch having a second hand. When the piston stops at top center give him the signal to count fifteen seconds at the end of which he is to open slightly the compression cock and listen for a hissing sound as air escapes. If a hissing sound is heard, test again, waiting twenty seconds. If no sound is heard at fifteen seconds test again at ten seconds.

7. For each cylinder make a record of the number of seconds during which it holds compression. Ten seconds may be considered " fair compression "; fifteen seconds " good " and twenty seconds or more " very good."

NOTE. Try the spark plugs with an end wrench to see if they are fitting tightly.

The most common causes of poor compression are leakage at the valves and in old engines leakage between the piston and the cylinder wall. Valve leakage is frequently due to pitted valve face or valve seat which may be corrected by grinding. Valve leakage may also be due to a weak valve spring or to warping of the valve.

46. COMPRESSION—B

MATERIALS. **Laboratory automobile engine and reference books.**

If the throttle is open the maximum compression for the common automobiles at top center at the end of the compression stroke should be between 70 and 100 lbs. per square inch. Engines that are designed for slow speed have low compressions and those designed for high speed have high compressions. When explosion occurs the pressure immediately increases to about 250 or 300 lbs. per square inch at the beginning of the power stroke. The initial pressure at explosion will depend upon the degree of compression and upon the proper proportioning of the mixture in the carburetor as well as the speed of the engine. A very lean or a very rich mixture explodes or burns slowly in the cylinder.

A. **Reference Work.** Use Dyke.

1. What are the advantages of high compression?

2. What are the disadvantages of high compression?

3. State the maximum compression for the following makes of cars—Hudson, Chalmers, Packard, Ford (see *Ford Supplement* for Ford).

4. What are the evidences of a hole in the cylinder wall?

5. An explosion from the engine through the intake manifold into the carburetor may indicate what compression defect? How may a very lean mixture produce a similar effect?

6. An explosion in the exhaust pipe and muffler may be due to what compression trouble? Can you suggest another method of getting an explosion in the exhaust pipe?

7. How may a piece of rubber hose be used for detecting a leak in the inlet or in the exhaust valves?

8. If piston rings are loose and allow an excess of oil to pass from the crankcase past the piston into the combustion chamber, what trouble is likely to result?

9. How may a valve seat be tested for leakage by the use of Prussian blue? by lead-pencil marks?

10. What is a compressometer?

11. How does high compression affect the flow of spark current between the terminals of the spark plug? Which has the higher resistance to the flow of the spark current—high compression or low compression?

12. What adjustment should be made at the spark points for very high compression?

13. If a spark plug just barely sparks when it is taken out and laid on the engine, does it necessarily follow that it will spark in the engine under operating conditions? Explain.

B. **Troubles.**

14. Refer to the classification of troubles in *The Gasoline Automobile* and list the common engine troubles which may be due to compression trouble.

47. TIRES—A

Manipulation

MATERIALS. Ford wheel with clincher rim; tire tools; tire pump; reference books.

A. **Removing a Clincher Tire from the Wheel.** Read *The Gasoline Automobile* on The Clincher One-piece Rim, including the directions for removing the tire.

(*a*) First jack up the wheel clear of the road. The valve cap should be unscrewed, the lock nut removed, the tire deflated, and

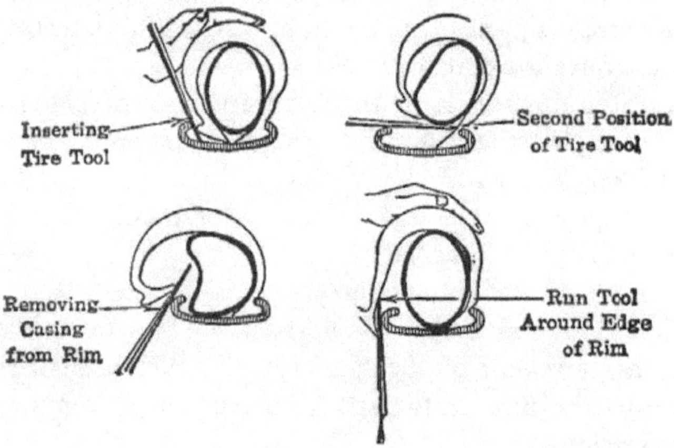

FIG. 50.—Method of removing tire from clincher rim.

the valve stem pushed into the rim. When this is done loosen up the bead of the shoe in the flange of the rim by working and pushing with the hands, then insert one of the tire irons or levers under the head. Special care must be taken in inserting the levers to avoid pinching or cutting the inner tube. The tire iron should be pushed in just far enough to get a good hold on the under side of the bead, but not so far as to pinch the inner tube between the rim and the tool. A second iron should be inserted in the same manner 7 or 8 inches from the first, and a third tool the same distance from the second. As a clincher tire must always be pried over the flange, two or three levers will be needed and the knee of the operator should be used to hold down one lever while the other two are being manipulated in working the tire clear of the rim. After freeing a length of the bead from the rim, the entire outer edge of the casing may be removed by the hands.

(*b*) Beginning at the point on the side of wheel diametrically opposite the valve pull out the inner tube carefully until all that remains in the casing is the section containing the valve. Remove the latter by inserting your hand in the casing and grasping the base of the valve firmly and lifting the valve out of the hole in the felloe of the wheel. It may then be removed from the casing in the same manner as the rest of the tube was removed. Remove the casing from the rim by levering the inner side of the casing over the outer flange of the rim in the same manner as before.

(*c*) Pump up the inner tube until it is well filled out for testing purposes and test it for leaks in a pan of water. Should there be a puncture, notify the instructor and show the exact location of the puncture. Test the valve for leakage in the same manner as in testing the tire.

(*d*) Inspect the casing for cuts or breaks. Pass your hand over the complete inner lining of the casing carefully, in order to ascertain whether or not any sharp particles (tacks, nails, pebbles, glass, etc.) have penetrated the casing.

1. Write a report on the condition of the casing and inner tube. Replace the tire on the rim, performing the operations in the reverse order from that used in taking it off. Get a pump from the instructor for pumping up the tire.

B. **Reference Work.** *The Gasoline Automobile; Motor Vehicles;* Dyke.

2. What is meant by *bead* of a tire?

3. What is the difference between a straight side tire and a clincher tire?

4. What causes "pinching" of the inner tube?

5. Why is talc or soapstone used between the inner tube and the casing?

6. How should inner tubes be carried in the car?

7. State the function of : (*a*) the bead filler, (*b*) the valve cap, (*c*) the tread, (*d*) the fabric, (*e*) the valve spring.

48. TIRES—B

Testing, Patching, and Vulcanizing Tires

MATERIALS. **Inner tube; pail; tube bag; cement and patches; five-minute vulcanizing apparatus.**

A. **Testing the Tire for a Puncture.** Ask the instructor for an inner tube. Test it for punctures by passing it through a pail of water. Place your finger over the puncture; if one is found, take the tube to the instructor. After he has examined it, deflate the tube by removing the valve plunger, roll up the tube, thus expelling all the air, and insert the valve plunger, screwing it firmly into its seat.

After drying the tube fold it in the correct manner (see *The Gasoline Automobile*), tie it together, place it in the bag, and return it to the instructor.

B. **Patching the Tube.** The instructor will supply you with another tube or section of tube and some patches. Make a hole in the tube with a nail and with cement or "cementless" patch repair this puncture, following the directions on the box.

1. Why is it necessary to clean the surface of the tube around the puncture with gasoline?

2. Why is it customary to roughen the surface with sandpaper?

3. Could all punctures be repaired in this way?

4. What advantage has this method of repairing over vulcanizing?

5. Does this method make the repair permanent?

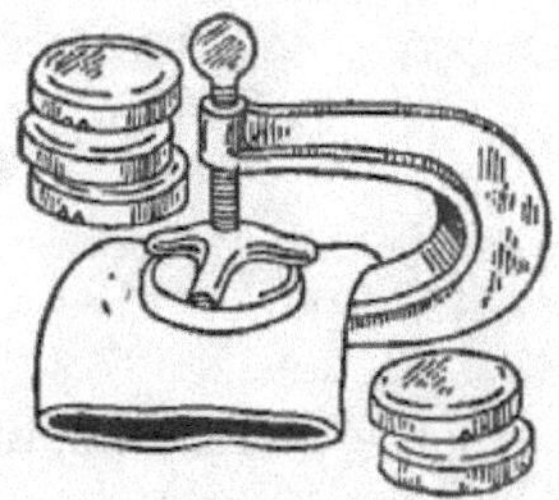

FIG. 51.—Five-minute vulcanizing set for inner tubes.

C. **Vulcanizing.** Repair another puncture by vulcanizing, using a small vulcanizer and the prepared patches.

The directions of the manufacturer should be followed explicitly, and in addition it may be necessary to direct a current of air from the tire pump on the inflammable cardboard after you have set fire to it. Otherwise it may burn very slowly or possibly go out.

6. Is this method of vulcanizing used by the expert repairman in repairing a blow-out?

7. What is the difference between a puncture and a blow-out?

8. Does this method of vulcanizing make a permanent repair?

9. If the outer cover or casing bursts on the road, what can be done?

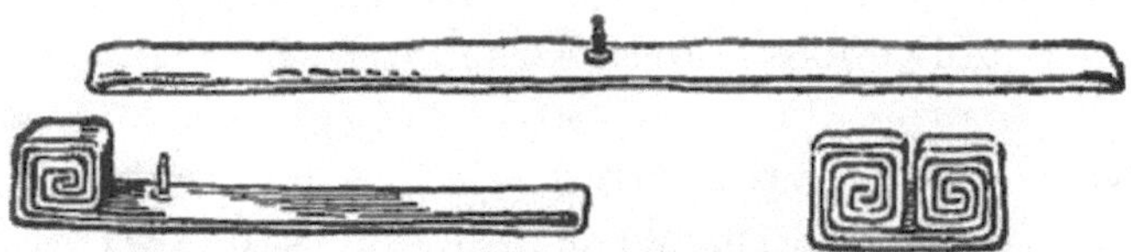

FIG. 52.—Proper method of folding inner tube.

D. **Care of Tires.**

10. Name at least six causes that lead to tire deterioration.

11. What precaution should be taken in regard to tires when storing a car for the winter?

12. Why is it essential to have the tire properly inflated at all times?

13. Name some of the enemies of rubber.

14. State some important points in caring for tires. See *The Gasoline Automobile.*

49. TIRES—C

Removing a Split-band Demountable Rim

MATERIALS. Laboratory automobile; wheel with split-band demountable rim.

(*a*) Remove one of the rear tires from the laboratory automobile by unscrewing the lugs which hold the detachable rim in place. Place the lugs on the running board of the car. (Why?) Roll the tire to a place where you have room to work on it. Deflate it by removing valve core or plunger.

(*b*) This rim is known as a "split" rim. In order to prevent it from opening a lock, or metal tab is riveted on the rim at the split. The rim is locked when this tab is in the longitudinal position and unlocked when it is in the transverse position.

(*c*) By means of a hammer unlock the rim and, with a rim compressor, contract the rim. In doing this place one claw of the tool diametrically opposite the split and the other claw close to the split.

(*d*) Now remove the tire from the rim, being careful not to injure the valve. If the casing should be rusted on, use one of the ordinary tire tools to loosen it. Remove the flap and inner tube from the casing and inspect the casing carefully for any defects.

(*e*) Carefully put the inner tube back into the casing and replace it on the rim, performing the operations in the reverse order of that given above. Do not forget to insert the flap and be sure that it fits properly to avoid a pinched tube. Pump up the tire before putting it back on the wheel. When it has been pumped to the proper pressure replace it on the wheel. Set all lugs and screws properly. Have the instructor inspect your work at this point.

1. What is the full name for this type of rim?

2. Describe the construction of two other kinds of demountable rims.

Fig. 53.—Operations in the removal of split-band type of rim from tire.

3. State the advantages of such rims?

4. What precaution should be taken when inflating the tire after it has been mounted?

5. What is the function of a flap?

6. Is there any advantage in changing the casings of tires from front to rear after they have been used for some time?

7. To what extent do "non-skid" casings prevent skidding?

8. Is a "non-skid" casing of any value when used on front wheels?

9. What is the best "non skid" device? What rules should be observed in its use?

50. CARBURETORS—C

Carburetor Adjustments

MATERIALS. Carburetors of various types, sectional carburetors.

When a carburetor is properly adjusted the mixture burns in the cylinder with a colorless or bluish flame. If it is very rich it burns with a yellow or smoky flame and tends to deposit carbon on spark plugs, cylinders, and pistons. If it is too lean the engine will show loss of power or "back fire" into the carburetor. For economical use of fuel the carburetor may be adjusted to supply a slightly lean mixture.

It is a common practice to begin the adjustment of a simple carburetor by decreasing the supply of gasoline until, in pulling a hill, the exploding mixture "back fires" into the carburetor as the engine, under load, decreases its speed. Then the proportion of gasoline is increased by very gradual steps until the engine pulls the hill without "back firing." Great care must be observed to avoid making the mixture too rich or richer than is necessary for economical operation. The mixture may be richer than necessary and yet show no visible evidence of richness.

The more complicated carburetors with compensating air and gasoline valves require special adjustments for the different speeds, low, intermediate, and high, and the adjustment of these carburetors should be taken up separately.

1. A very lean mixture burns slowly. Explain how this sometimes results in an explosion in the carburetor (back firing) when the engine runs slowly.

2. If the mixture is slightly lean, why does opening the throttle suddenly sometimes cause "back firing" into the carburetor?

3. What sometimes causes "back firing" into the carburetor in going up a steep hill just before shifting gears?

4. If the engine should "back fire" and ignite the gasoline in the carburetor, what should be done immediately to avoid burning up the car?

5. What are some means of obtaining rich mixtures for starting?

6. If a priming cup is opened at the time of explosion, what should be the color of the flame which shoots out?

7. In using low-grade gasoline, how does applying heat to the carburetor and to the intake manifold aid carburetion?

8. Why does an engine run better when it is warmed up?

9. What kind of mixture produces a large percentage of the deadly gas—carbon monoxide?

10. If the exhaust does not smoke at low speed and does smoke at high speed, what adjustment is needed?

11. What sometimes causes an engine to smoke badly at the time of starting?

12. What would be the effect of a leak in the manifold at some point between the carburetor and the cylinder? Old engines sometimes leak around the intake-valve stems.

13. If the engine runs for a short time and stops, then runs for a short time and stops again, what may be the cause?

14. If a carburetor begins flooding slowly after the engine stops, what may be the cause?

15. Carburetor adjustments should not be changed until other possible troubles are carefully investigated. What other tests should be made before changes are made on the carburetor adjustment?

51. CARBURETORS—D

Carburetor Adjustments (*Continued*)

MATERIALS. Carburetors—Schebler Model E, Kingston Model E, and Holley Model G.

The many types of compensating devices and special adjustments on the various makes of carburetors are all designed to keep the proportions of the air and gasoline vapor constant with variations in engine speed. The common adjustments are for low and high

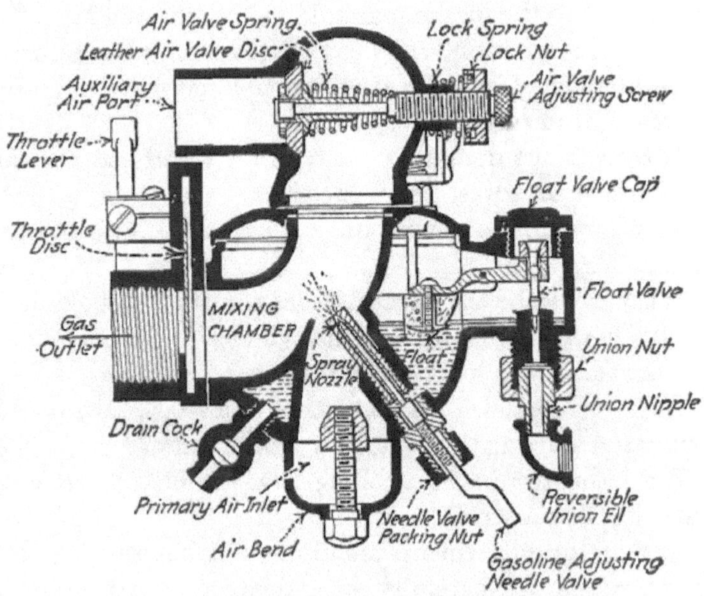

FIG. 54.—Schebler Model E Carburetor.

speeds. If the carburetor contains a simple spray needle and a simple auxiliary air valve, the spray needle is set for low-speed adjustment and the auxiliary air valve is set to open at higher speeds and supply the increased amount of air necessary to keep the mixture properly balanced.

A. **The Schebler Model E.** Use sectional carburetor, Schebler Model E, manufacturer's circular, or illustration in *Motor Vehicles*.

1. Is this carburetor design concentric or eccentric?
2. By what type of adjustment is the gasoline controlled?
3. Where does the air for the low-speed adjustment enter the carburetor?
4. Where does the additional air for the high-speed adjustment enter this carburetor?

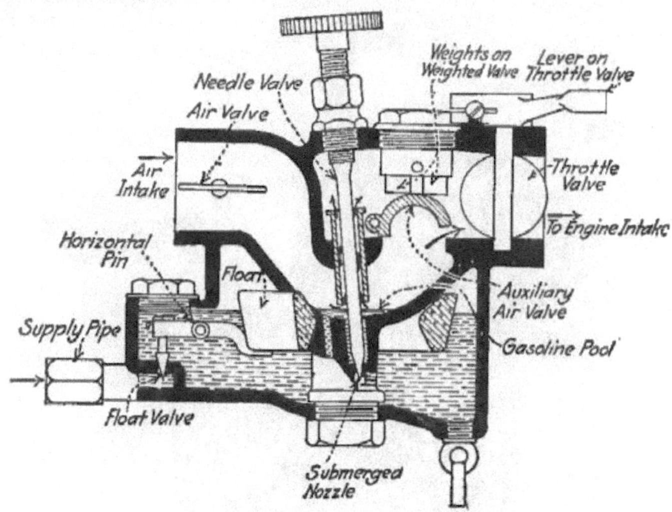

Fig. 55.—Kingston Model E carburetor.

5. At what point does the mixture pass out of this carburetor?
6. What keeps the auxiliary air valve shut at low speeds?
7. What would be the effect upon the engine if the auxiliary air-valve spring tension were too loose or if the auxiliary air valve were held open at low speed?
8. Give directions for making the low-speed adjustment. See *Motor Vehicles*.
9. Give directions for making the high-speed adjustment.
10. What is the function of the "air-valve adjusting screw"?
11. What is the function of the "lock nut" and "lock spring"?

12. Explain the sequence of operations which result in opening the auxiliary air valve when the throttle is opened. Is this valve pulled open from the inside or pushed open from the outside?

B. **The Kingston Model E.** See *Motor Vehicles.*

13. Is this carburetor concentric or eccentric?

14. How does the position of the spray-needle in this instrument differ from that in the Schebler Model E?

Fig. 56.—Holley Model G carburetor.

15. What is the function of the cup or puddle above the spray-needle valve? This carburetor represents the "puddle type."

16. In this carburetor how is the auxiliary air for high speeds supplied?

17. How many balls are used? Why are they placed at different depths?

The Kingston Model L, similar in principle to the Kingston Model E, was designed for and used for many years on Ford cars.

C. **The Holley Models G and H.** See *The Gasoline Automobile.* These carburetors have no auxiliary air valve.

18. What is the function of the low-speed tube in the Holley models?

52. CARBURETORS—E

The Stromberg Plain Tube and the Zenith Model L

MATERIALS. Stromberg Plain Tube, and Zenith Model L carburetors; instruction books and reference books.

A. **The Stromberg Plain Tube.** This is a plain-tube carburetor. A number of the leading manufacturers are now making "plain-tube" carburetors. In this type gasoline sprays into the Venturi from small holes either in the walls of the Venturi, as in the Stromberg, or in the nozzle housing, as in the Schebler. The gasoline tube leading to the Venturi is "air-bled," having an opening which admits air into the gasoline tube before it sprays into the Venturi opening. With higher speeds and increased suction a larger proportion of air enters the gasoline tube, thus reducing the proportion of gasoline and keeping the mixture properly balanced. With the reduced flow of gasoline at high speeds no auxiliary air valve is necessary.

If a sectional model of the Stromberg plain-tube carburetor is available, examine it. Use, as a reference, *Motor Vehicles.*

1. When the throttle is closed, as in idling, what causes gasoline to rise in the idling tube to the idling jet?

2. When the engine is idling, why does gasoline not flow out by the idling adjustment screw into the mixing chamber below the throttle?

3. In idling, what does flow by the idling adjustment screw?

4. If the idling adjustment screw were screwed in further, what effect would be produced upon the idling speed?

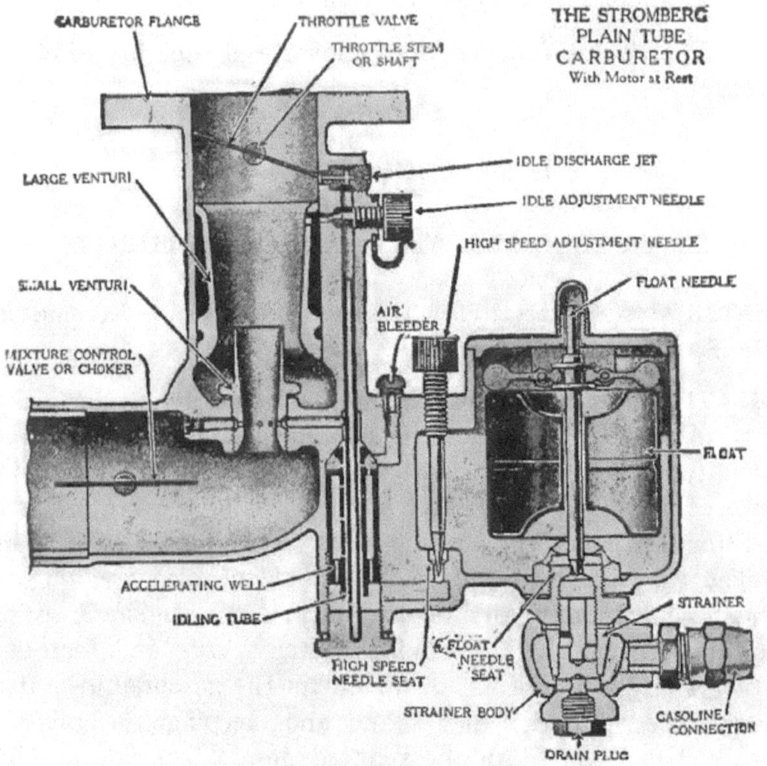

FIG. 57.—Stromberg plain-tube carburetor.

5. In running at the higher speeds, how does air get into the gasoline tube before it reaches the holes in the Venturi?

6. Under what conditions of operating the engine does air pass from the bleeder tube down into the accelerating well?

7. Where is the high-speed adjustment screw located?

8. Give directions for making the high-speed adjustment. See *Motor Vehicles*.

B. **The Zenith Model L.** See *Motor Vehicles.*

9. What difficulty occurs in the use of a single-nozzle carburetor with varying speeds?

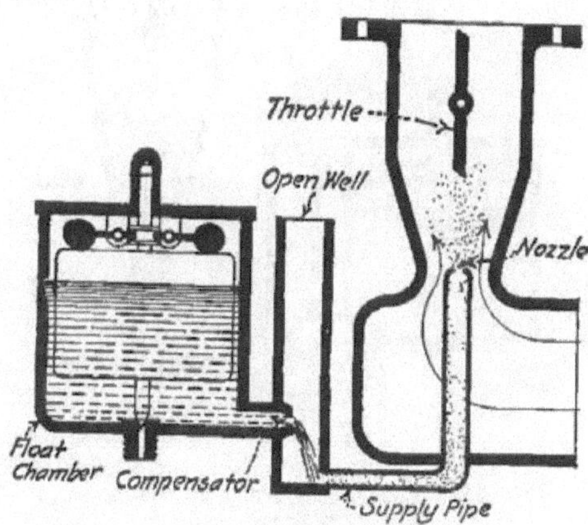

FIG. 58.—Constant-flow nozzle.

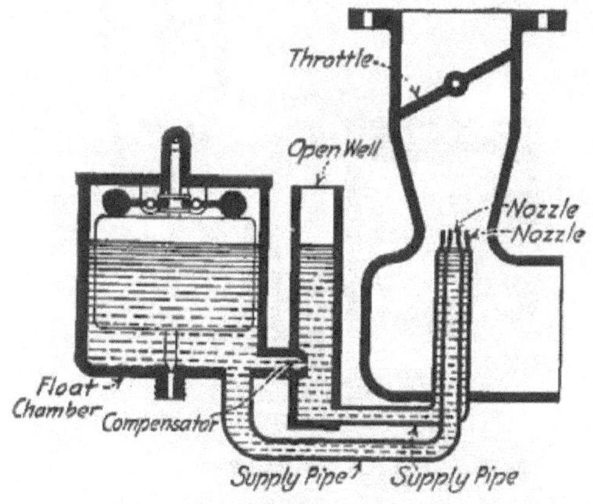

FIG. 59.—Zenith compound jet with engine standing still.

10. How does the Zenith correct for this trouble?

11. Under what condition of engine speed is the larger proportion of gasoline furnished by (*a*) the center nozzle, (*b*) the outer nozzle?

12. What is meant by the expression "compensation" as applied to this carburetor?

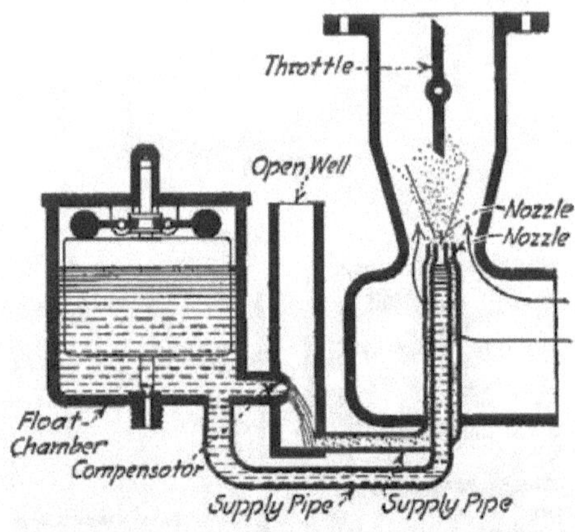

FIG. 60.—Zenith carburetor at low speed.

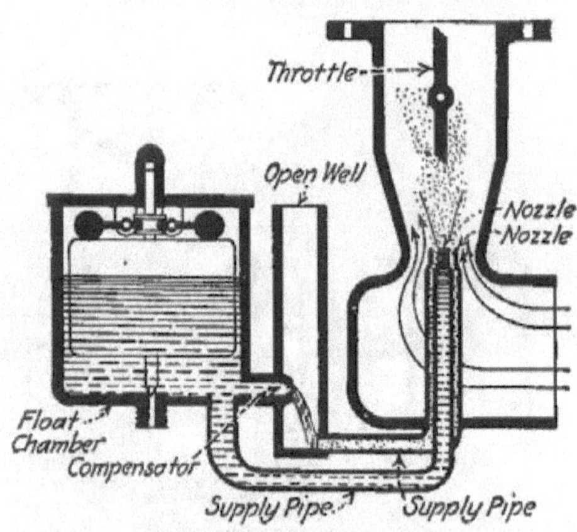

FIG. 61.—Zenith carburetor at high speed.

13. If the mixture is too lean at high speed which orifice should be made larger?

14. Explain how gasoline is supplied in starting the engine.

15. Explain how gasoline is supplied for idling.

53. CARBURETORS—F

Reference Works *Motor Vehicles* **and** *The Gasoline Automobile*

MATERIALS. Carburetors of various types; manufacturers' instruction sheets and reference books.

A. The Rayfield Model G. This carburetor has three air inlets and two gasoline inlets. One of the air inlets is a constant opening

Fig. 62.—Section of Rayfield Model G carburetor.

in the side of the carburetor leading directly to the spray-nozzle; another is the upper automatic air valve; and a third is a butterfly valve (lower air valve) which is controlled by the upper automatic air valve and which opens when the upper air valve opens. One gasoline inlet is the spray-nozzle, the other the metering pin.

Two adjustments are provided, high speed and low speed. Both adjustments are on the spray-nozzle. The low-speed adjustment sets the spray-nozzle as in any simple carburetor. The throttle mechanism connects with the spray-nozzle pin, causing the spray-nozzle to open wider as the throttle opens for high speed. This mechanism contains the high-speed adjustment screw.

1. For what speed does the carburetor depend chiefly upon the constant air opening?

2. For what speed does the carburetor depend chiefly upon the upper and the lower air valves?

3. What causes the metering-pin nozzle to open and supply gasoline?

4. What keeps the upper automatic air valve closed at low speed?

5. What opens the lower air valve?

6. What is the function of a dash-pot piston on an air valve?

7. How is this carburetor equipped for warming the mixture?

8. Explain the purpose and operation of the dash control on the Rayfield.

9. Give directions for making the high-speed adjustment on the Rayfield.

B. **The Marvel—Buick.** This carburetor contains a spray needle, an auxiliary air valve, and a high-speed nozzle.

10. What type of auxiliary air valve has this carburetor?

11. Explain the operation of the high-speed nozzle.

C. **The Tillotson—Overland.**

12. Explain briefly the regulation of the air supply in the Tillotson.

D. **The Packard.**

13. Does this carburetor contain a spray needle?

14. How is compensation provided for in this carburetor?

15. What provision is made for keeping the mixture warm?

E. **The Pierce-Arrow.**

16. State (*a*) type of float chamber, (*b*) type of spray-nozzle, (*c*) type of auxiliary air inlet.

F. **The Cadillac.**

17. State the function of (*a*) the "gas saver," (*b*) the throttle pump, (*c*) the automatic throttle.

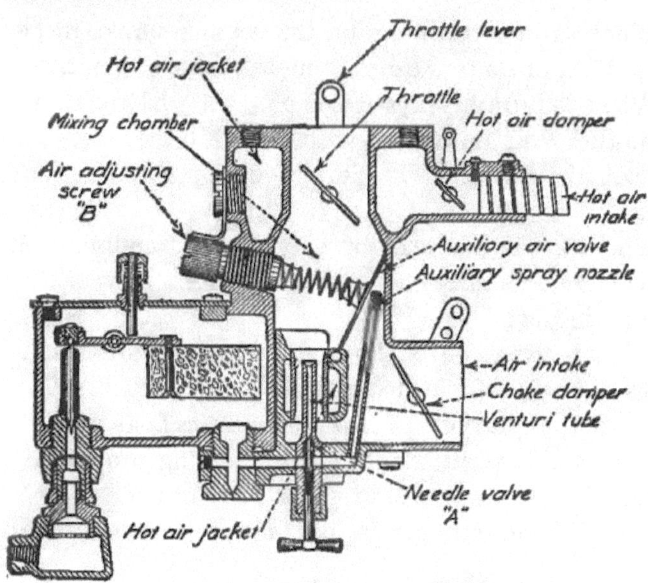

FIG. 63.—The Marvel Model E carburetor.

G. **The Stewart.**

18. State the function of (*a*) the metering pin, (*b*) the valve A.

H. **The Hudson.**

19. What causes the piston to rise?
20. What controls the size of opening at the spray-nozzle?

54. FUEL FEED SYSTEMS

MATERIALS. Ford chassis with tank and feed pipe; laboratory automobile with fuel system attached; sectional demonstration model of the Stewart Vacuum Tank, or diagrams; manufacturers' circulars.

A. **Gravity Feed Systems.** See textbooks.

1. What is the meaning of the expression "Gravity Feed System"? Name a make of automobile which uses it.
2. When the gravity system is used, in what relative position must the fuel tank be located with regard to the level of the float chamber of the carburetor? State two common locations for the fuel tank.
3. Examine the fuel tank on a typical automobile. State the function of: (*a*) the tank cover, (*b*) the shutoff valve, (*c*) sediment cup and drain plug.
4. What is the advantage of partitions in the fuel tank?
5. Should a fuel tank be closed air tight? Explain.
6. State the purpose of the carburetor float needle. What carburetor trouble results from its not seating properly?
7. How is the gasoline shut off at the Ford fuel tank?
8. State two advantages in locating the fuel tank in the cowl.

B. **Pressure Feed System.** Many cars are now being constructed with fuel tanks attached to the rear end of the frame at a point lower than the level of the carburetor float-chamber. In this arrangement it is necessary to use either a pressure system or a vacuum system for raising the fuel to the carburetor. The simplest form of pressure system provides for pumping air into the fuel tank above the gasoline, forcing the gasoline out through a pipe in the bottom of the tank to the carburetor. For this purpose an air pump may be operated by the engine, the hand pump being used only for starting.

9. What advantage is obtained with this system in regard to feed as compared with the gravity system?

FIG. 64.—Gravity gasoline supply system on Ford car—supply tank under front seat.

10. State some other advantages in placing the fuel tank at the rear of the frame.

11. What is the purpose of a safety valve in this system?

12. State some sources of trouble in a pressure system.

C. **The Stewart Vacuum System.** In this system the gasoline

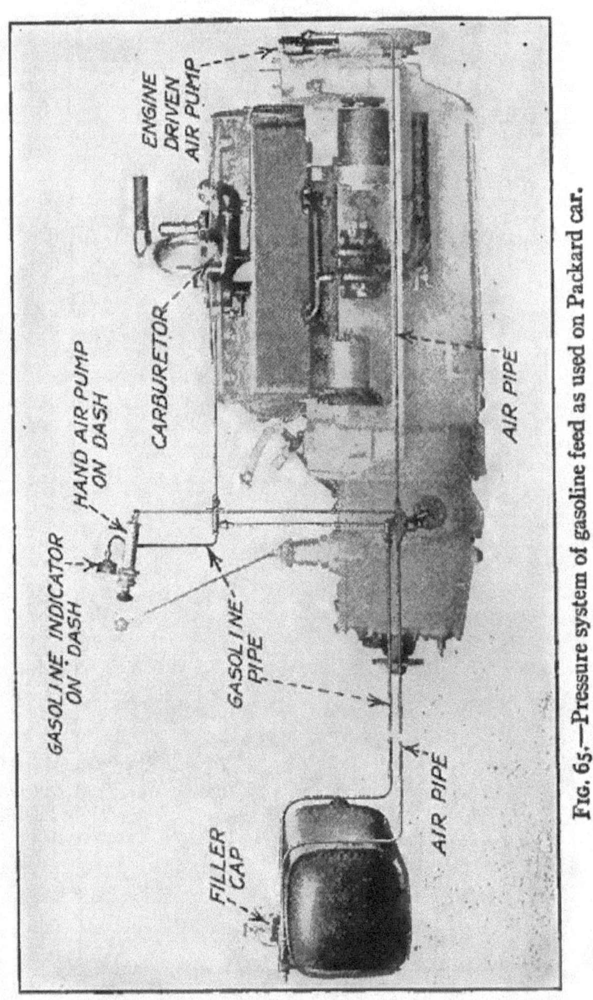

Fig. 65.—Pressure system of gasoline feed as used on Packard car.

is drawn from the tank at the rear, by suction, obtained from the intake manifold of the engine. The gasoline is drawn into a somewhat complicated " vacuum tank " which is placed on the engine side of the dash and from which the gasoline flows by gravity to the carburetor. If a sectional model of this tank is available

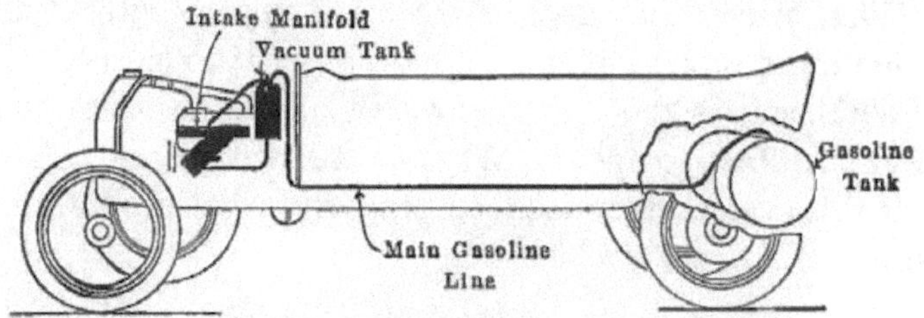

FIG. 66.—Vacuum system of gasoline supply.

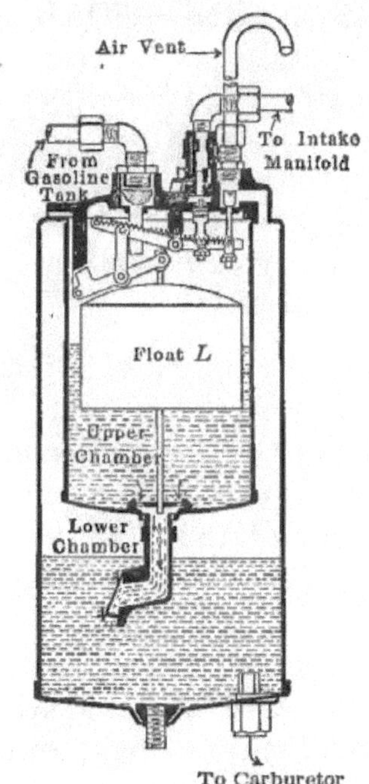

FIG. 67.—Stewart vacuum tank.

examine it carefully. Read the description of the Stewart Vacuum Tank in *The Gasoline Automobile* and in *Motor Vehicles.*

13. What causes a condition of suction or a partial vacuum in the pipe leading to the intake manifold?

14. What causes the valve between the upper chamber and the intake manifold pipe to open? What causes it to close?

15. What causes the "flapper valve" between the upper and the lower chambers to open? What causes it to close?

16. If this system does not feed properly, what are the probable causes? See *Motor Vehicles.*

55. VALVE TIMING—FORD ENGINE

MATERIALS. Ford engine, ruler, and piece of chalk.

A. Read the discussion of valve timing in the *Model T Ford Car.* The timing of the Ford valves is given in terms of the distance which the piston moves instead of in degrees as is commonly done with gas engines.

1. The opening and the closing of the inlet and the exhaust valves is usually given as a certain number of degrees before or after top-center position or bottom-center position of the piston. How many degrees constitute a complete circle?

2. The circumference of the Ford flywheel is 46.5 inches. One inch on the outside of the flywheel, therefore, equals how many degrees?

B. Time the inlet valves of cylinders No. 3 and 4 in degrees as follows: Locate the inlet valve by its position in relation to the intake manifold. When the piston reaches top-center place a chalk mark on the flywheel at a point opposite a chalk mark on the top coil of the generator. Now watch the inlet valve and slowly move the flywheel beyond top-center until you first notice the inlet valve beginning to open.

3. Measure in inches on the flywheel how far the chalk mark has moved past top-center and state this in degrees. This is the opening time for the inlet valve.

4. When the piston reaches bottom-center of the intake stroke make another chalk mark and measure how far past bottom-center the mark has moved when the inlet valve has finished closing. State in degrees the time of closing of the inlet valve.

C. Time the exhaust valves of the same cylinders in a similar manner. When the exhaust valve begins to open make a chalk mark on the flywheel. When the piston reaches bottom-center measure the distance moved in inches.

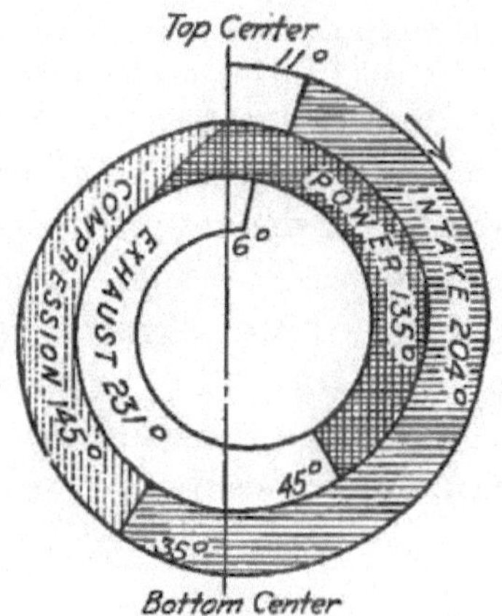

Fig. 68.—Valve timing of the average engine.

5. State in degrees the time of opening of the exhaust valve.

6. Determine the time of closing of the exhaust valve on the Ford.

7. How does this timing of the Ford compare with the timing of the average automobile engine? See valve-timing diagram, Fig. 68. Make a corresponding diagram for the Ford engine.

8. What clearance should exist between the valve stem and the push rod?

9. How would too much clearance affect the timing?

10. If the clearance is too small, what trouble may result?

11. How must the large and small time gears mesh when the valves are properly timed?

12. Explain the timing marks frequently found on engine flywheels. See Dyke.

56. IGNITION TIMING

Checking the Ignition Timing on the Laboratory Engines

MATERIALS. One and one-half horsepower gas engine on truck; engine of one of the standard automobiles with battery ignition; Ford engine.

With the spark lever retarded the spark in an engine cylinder should occur at top-center at the end of the compression stroke. As the engine increases in speed the spark should be advanced in order to get the maximum power. Ignition timing involves the setting of the ignition mechanisms of the timer, the distributor, and the spark lever so that when the spark lever is in the retarded position the spark occurs at top-center of the compression stroke and when the spark lever is advanced the spark occurs before the piston reaches top-center of compression.

A. **Laboratory Gas Engine.**

1. Has this engine any device for advancing or retarding the spark?

2. At what time with respect to top-center of the compression stroke does ignition occur?

3. How may the ignition time of this engine be adjusted?

B. **Automobile Engine.** Check the ignition timing of this engine. Read *Motor Vehicles* and *The Gasoline Automobile* on

Ignition Timing. Open all priming cocks except on cylinder No. 1 and place the spark lever in the extreme retarded position. Examine the flywheel to see if it contains timing marks. See Dyke. These marks may be used to determine the top-center of cylinders No. 1 and No. 4. Top-center position in some engines may be determined by removing a spark plug and placing a stick into the spark plug opening against the top of the piston. When the stick reaches the highest point as the engine is turned over the piston is on top-center.

4. Why should the spark lever be in the retarded position when the engine is timed?

5. In timing the engine, when should the contact points cf the timer separate?

6. If the contact points of the timer should not separate at the proper time, what adjustment might be necessary?

7. What is the danger in cranking an engine by hand when the spark is advanced?

8. What troubles occur when an engine is operated with spark too far advanced? See Dyke.

9. Through how many degrees does the mechanism usually permit the spark to advance?

10. How does the timer mechanism provide for advancing the spark?

11. How would you determine the firing order of the engine?

12. How could you determine the direction of rotation of the distributor arm?

13. How does an automatic spark advance mechanism operate?

C. **The Ford Engine.**

14. How can top-center of cylinder No. 1 be determined without removing the cylinder head?

15. With spark retarded, in what position should the piston of the Ford be when the spark occurs?

16. What should be the position of the timer roller when the spark occurs in question 15?

17. Describe the Ford spark advance mechanism.

57. DIFFERENTIAL—A. BEVEL GEARS

The Differential Mechanism and the Final Gears

MATERIALS. Small Meccano toy model; large laboratory automobile chassis, and reference books.

Examine the small model of a differential. Note that one wheel may revolve while the other stands still, or one wheel may go

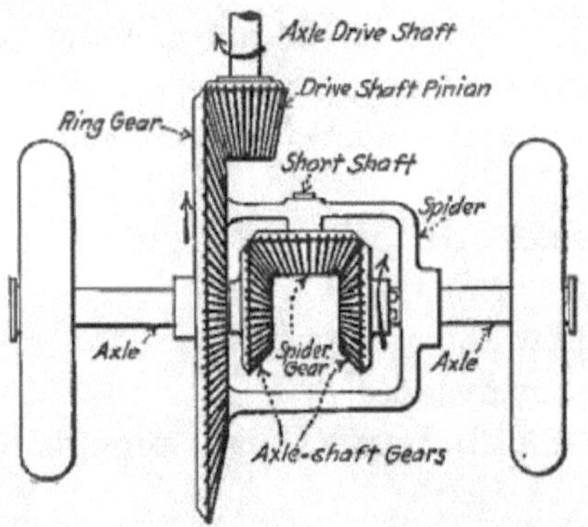

FIG. 69.—Simplified illustration of the differential gears.

forward while the other revolves in the opposite direction. Let one person hold one rear wheel of the laboratory automobile while the other turns the opposite wheel. Note that the differential permits both wheels to revolve in the same direction either at the same rate or at different rates.

1. State why a differential is needed in the operation of an automobile. See *Motor Vehicles*.

2. In what position on the automobile is the differential usually located?

3. Name one other position where it is sometimes located. See Dyke.

4. Describe the position of the following parts of a bevel gear differential mechanism: (*a*) differential housing, (*b*) drive-shaft pinion, (*c*) ring gear or driving gear, (*d*) spider gears, (*e*) axle-shaft gears.

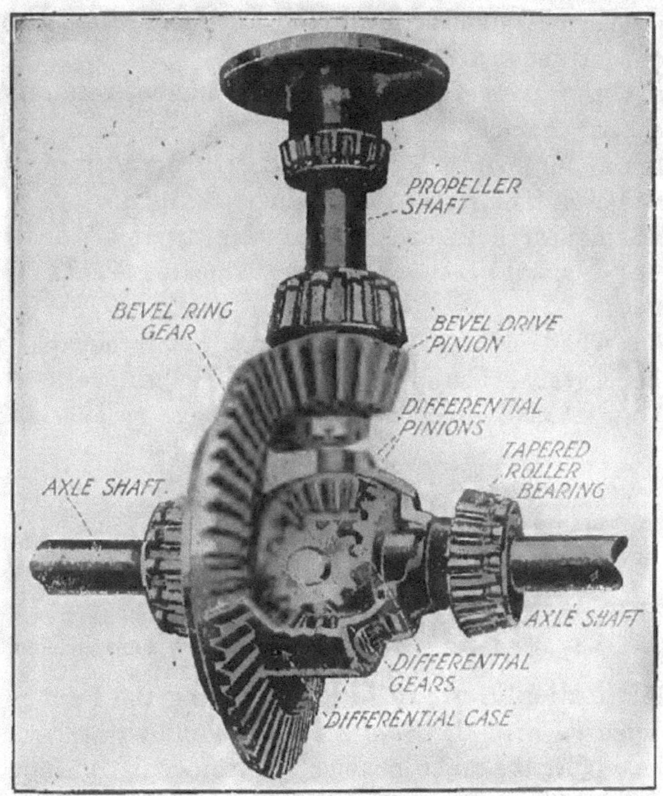

Fig. 70.—Differential gears.

5. Make a diagram showing the parts mentioned in No. 4 and label the parts.

6. Explain the purpose or function of each part mentioned in No. 4.

7. In the laboratory automobile differential mechanism how many axle shaft gears are used? How many spider gears?

8. Does the propeller shaft move if one wheel goes forward and the other backward at the same rate? Explain.

9. If one wheel stands still and the other goes forward must the propeller shaft move?

10. If both wheels go forward, but at different rates, must the propeller shaft move?

11. If the automobile is moving straight ahead do the spider gears revolve on their respective bearings? Explain.

12. Distinguish between the following types of final drive: (*a*) bevel, (*b*) spiral bevel gear, (*c*) worm gear. See *The Gasoline Automobile.*

13. For what reason is the spiral bevel gear preferable to the simple bevel gear? The spiral type is more expensive.

14. To what kind of service is the worm gear well adapted?

58. DIFFERENTIAL—B

Disassembling the Ford Rear Axle

MATERIALS. Ford rear axle mounted on a stand; tools; reference books.

For information in regard to disassembling the Ford rear axle and differential read the *Ford Manual.* Follow the instructions carefully. Note the order in which the various parts are removed. Place all parts in order on newspapers. Proceed slowly. When fully disassembled have your work approved by the instructor.

Caution. Do not use a hammer or attempt to force any part of the mechanism without first consulting the instructor.

For reference use *Motor Vehicles* and *The Model T Ford Car.*

1. Name three common types of differential. To which type does the Ford belong?

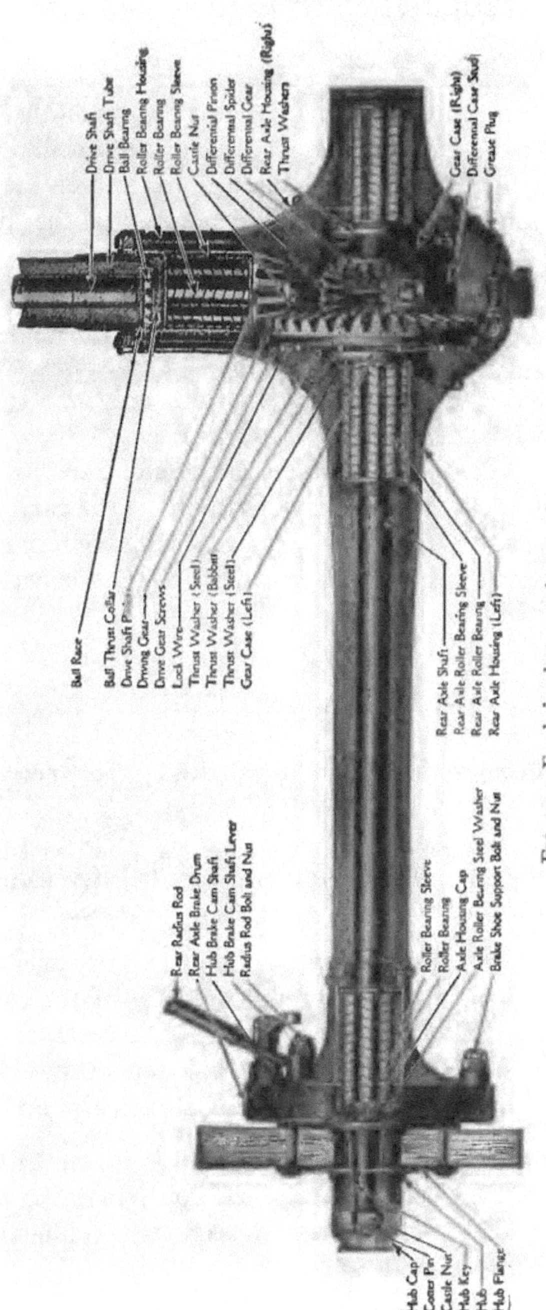

FIG. 71.—Ford simple type of rear axle.

2. Name the parts of a Ford differential.

3. What is meant by differential gear reduction?

4. What is the differential gear ratio of the Ford? Count the number of teeth on the propeller shaft pinion and on the ring gear.

5. What kind of lubricant should be used in the differential? How often should the lubricant be renewed?

6. How is the lubricant put into the differential? How can it be drawn off? See *Ford Manual.*

7. What type of bearings is found in the Ford rear axle?

8. Would the differential operate with only one spider gear? Why does the Ford use three?

9. When one rear wheel is on firm ground and the other in a mudhole, why is it sometimes difficult to move the car?

10. Explain as clearly as you can how the differential mechanism produces an equal pull on each rear wheel when the car is running on the road.

59. ALTERNATING CURRENTS

NOTE. This experiment should be preceded by the experiments on the electric motor and the electric generator.

MATERIALS. Pocket compass; large steel file, 1 inch wide by 10 inches long, magnetized; telephone magneto; battery voltmeter; electric bell; dry cell. Two coils of insulated copper wire of 1,000 turns each.

A. **Introductory Experiments.** Connect two insulated wires each 3 feet in length to the terminals of one of the coils. Place the coil on the table in position so that it lies with opening horizontal. Set the pocket compass on the top of the coil. Place the coil in such position that its opening stands east and west.

1. Touch the free ends of the two wires to the two terminals of a dry cell. Does the needle on the coil remain parallel to the wires of the coil? What position does it take while the dry cell current is flowing through the coil?

2. What effect is produced upon a coil by a current passing through it?

3. What causes the compass needle to change its position when a current passes through the coil? State the law which applies to the attraction and repulsion of magnetic poles.

4. How can you reverse the direction of current flow through the coil?

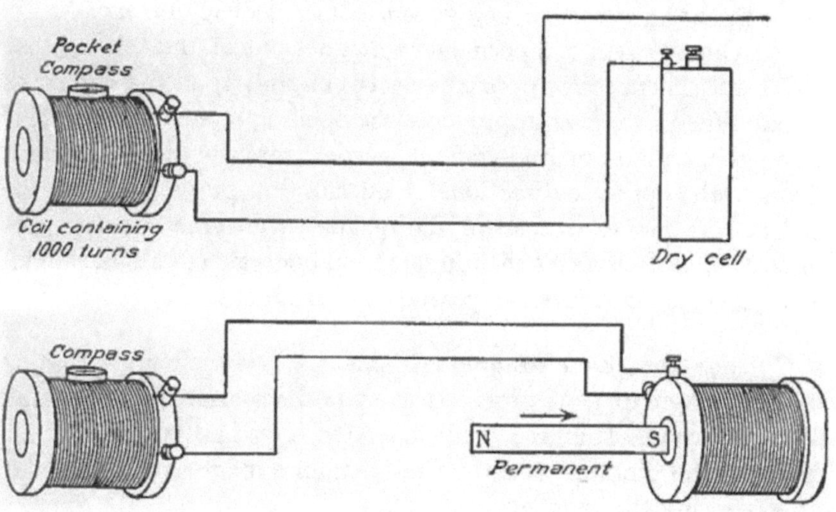

From Good's "Laboratory Projects in Physics." Used by permission of the Macmillan Company, publishers

FIG. 72.—Apparatus and wiring for the study of alternating currents.

5. What effect has this upon the polarity of the coil?

6. When the current through the coil is reversed, how is the position of the north pole of the compass affected? Observe closely. By reversing the flow of this dry cell current you produce the effect of an alternating current upon the coil. An alternating current flows first in one direction, then in the opposite direction.

7. How does an alternating current differ from a direct current in its magnetic effect upon a coil through which it is flowing?

B. **Alternating Currents Produced Mechanically.** Remove the dry cell and connect the two coils together by means of two 3-foot wires. Pass a large permanent magnet (magnetized large steel file) quickly into the coil just attached and observe the effect upon the compass on the other coil.

8. What evidence have you that this magnetism cutting through the turns of the coil generated an electric current?

9. Quickly pull the permanent magnet out of the coil. What effect did this produce upon the other coil and upon the compass?

10. When a magnet approaches the opening of a coil the current flows in one direction and when it recedes from the coil the current flows in the opposite direction. How can you prove this? If the coil of wire moves instead of the magnet, the same effect is produced. This illustrates the fundamental operation of all mechanically generated currents in dynamos and magnetos.

C. **The Telephone Magneto.** This is a low-tension alternating current magneto generator. It is sometimes used in telephones for the purpose of ringing the bell. Attach a small voltage electric lamp to the binding posts of the telephone magneto and light it by operating the magneto.

11. How is the magnetic field supplied in this magneto?

Note that one end of the wire winding is attached to the armature shaft which is insulated from the armature bearing. A spring conductor touches the end of the armature shaft and connects it by means of a wire to one of the binding posts of the magneto. The other end of the winding is attached to the ring on the armature shaft.

12. What prevents the current from passing from the armature shaft to the metal ring surrounding the shaft without passing through the lamp?

13. What prevents the current from passing from the metal

spring which is in contact with the armature shaft to the metal ring surrounding the shaft without passing through the lamp?

14. Does this magneto deliver a direct or an alternating current?

15. What change would be necessary in order to make an alternating-current magneto into a direct-current magneto?

16. Diagram the correct positions of the coil between the poles of the field magnet to satisfy the following conditions:

(*a*) When the direction of current in the armature coil changes. See *Motor Vehicles.*

(*b*) When the strength of the induced current is increasing.

(*c*) When the strength of the induced current is decreasing.

(*d*) When the voltage of the induced current is a maximum.

(*e*) When there is no current flowing.

60. IGNITION MAGNETOS—LOW-TENSION

The Remy Low-tension Magneto and the Ford Magneto

NOTE. Experiment 59, Alternating Currents, should precede this experiment.

MATERIALS. Automobile magneto, Ford ignition system (Ford demonstration car); dry cells; ring stands; wire.

Dry-cell current for automobile ignition purposes is expensive and not always dependable. Magnetos for ignition purposes were developed to eliminate these troubles. Magnetos may be divided into two classes,—the armature coil type in which the coil of wire is revolved between the poles of a permanent magnet, and the rotor type in which the coil is stationary and the rotor causes the magnetic field to vary in the coil. Low-tension magnetos produce low-voltage currents. High-tension magnetos produce high-voltage currents.

A. **The Remy Low-tension Magneto.** Study the Remy or some other low-tension magneto in the laboratory. This magneto is of the rotor type. Read carefully *The Gasoline Automobile* or

Motor Vehicles on the rotor type of magneto. If but one winding is used, the resulting voltage will be low, therefore it is called a

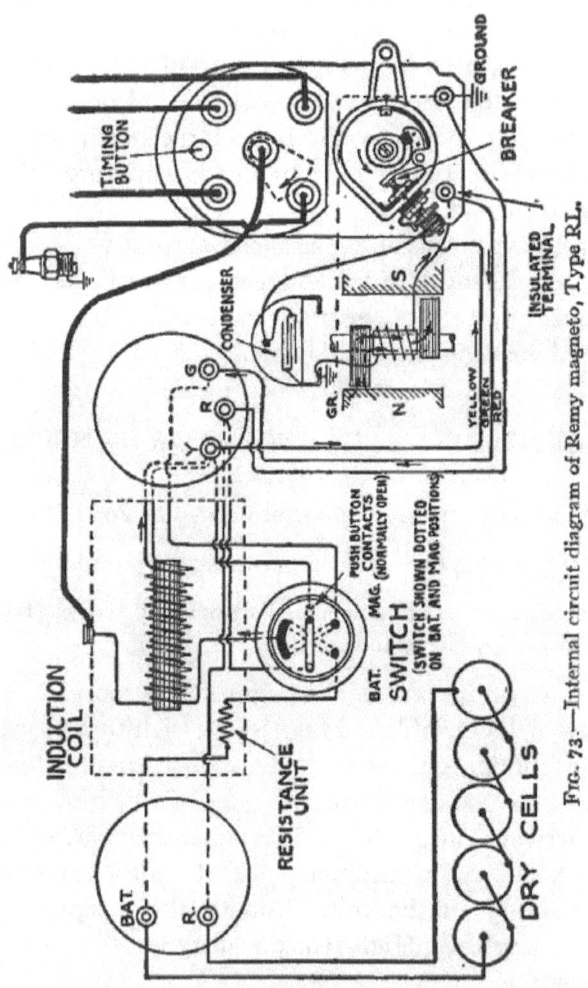

FIG. 73.—Internal circuit diagram of Remy magneto, Type RL.

low-tension magneto. A high-tension magneto has both a primary and a secondary winding. Examine, if possible, a cross-section of a high-tension magneto. Note the primary and secondary windings. With a low-tension magneto an induction coil is necessary for producing the high-tension current for ignition.

1. What is the function of the rotor arms in this type of magneto? See *Motor Vehicles* or *The Gasoline Automobile.*

2. Of what material are the arms made? Why?

3. Does the coil in a rotor type of magneto revolve? Explain how a current is induced in this coil.

4. In what position of the rotor arms does the maximum number of lines of magnetic force pass through the coil? Make a diagram. See *Motor Vehicles.*

5. Explain how the direction of magnetic lines of force is reversed in the coil.

B. **The Ford Magneto.** The Ford magneto generates an alternating-current. Study the Ford ignition system on the demonstration car in the laboratory. Read *Motor Vehicles* and *The Gasoline Automobile* on the Ford magneto.

6. To what type of magneto does the Ford magneto belong—low-tension or high-tension?

7. How many coils does the Ford magneto have? Where are they located?

8. How many magnets does the Ford magneto have? Where are they located? What is their shape?

9. Diagram the magnetic field through two of the coils when a north pole of one of the magnets is opposite one of the coils and the south pole of the magnet is opposite an adjacent coil. See *The Gasoline Automobile.*

10. What part of a revolution must the flywheel make before the direction of the magnetic lines of force through the coils will change?

11. How does this changing of direction of the magnetic lines of force affect the current induced in the coils?

12. How many times is the direction of the current reversed while the flywheel makes one revolution?

13. What use does the Ford car make of the current which is generated by the magneto?

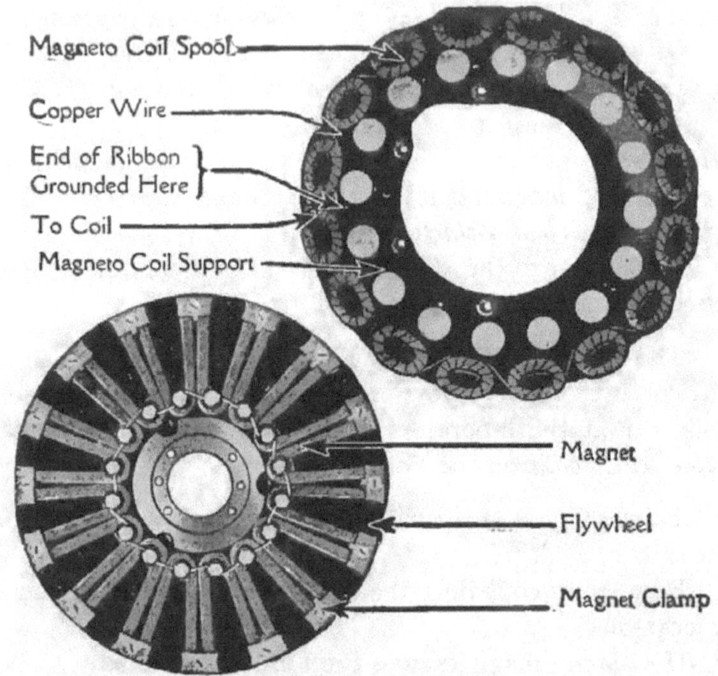

FIG. 74.—The Ford magneto.

14. Is it possible to use this current for charging a storage battery? Why?

NOTE. For the High-tension magneto see Ignition Systems—F.

61. AUTOMOBILE ELECTRIC CIRCUITS—C

The Starting, Charging, Ignition, and Lighting Circuits

MATERIALS. Electric generator used in the experiment on the electric generator; electric motor; storage battery; battery ammeter; two switches; induction coil; spark plug; telegraph sounder adapted to show the principle of the automatic cut-out; a standard type of automobile cut-out; wires.

With the apparatus found in the cabinet wire up on a table a complete automobile wiring system, showing the operation of the charging system, the starting system, the ignition system, and the lighting system, including the automatic cut-out in the charging system, the ammeter, the storage battery, the ignition switch, and the starting switch. Have the work approved by the instructor before the apparatus is taken down.

1. Make a copy of the diagram of the typical automobile wiring system. See Fig. 27. What is meant by the so-called single-wire system? What are some of the advantages of the single-wire system? See *Motor Vehicles*.

A. **The Starting Circuit.**

2. Does the current which operates the starting motor pass through the ammeter? Explain.

3. With a 6-volt storage battery about how many amperes are required to turn over an ordinary automobile engine?

4. What effect would this amount of current have upon an ordinary instrument board ammeter?

5. Name four uses for electric current which is registered on the ammeter at the instrument board.

B. **The Charging Circuit.**

6. At about what speed of the car does the generator begin to charge the storage battery?

7. What electrical mechanism connected with the generator prevents the storage-battery current from flowing through the generator when the generator is standing still or running slowly?

8. Why should the generator not be connected with the storage battery at low speed?

C. **The Ignition Circuits.**

9. From what source does the ignition current come when the engine is being started?

10. From what source does the ignition current come when the engine is running at speeds greater than about ten miles per hour?

11. What causes the direction of the current to change at higher speeds?

12. On the automobile, what shows that this change takes place?

13. Name the parts of the apparatus through which the ignition current flows at low speed.

14. Name the parts of the apparatus through which the ignition current flows at high speed.

15. State the advantages of an ammeter in the electrical system.

16. What part of the ignition circuit of an automobile causes the ignition current to flow intermittently?

17. Does the ammeter register current used for ignition when the engine is running at high speed? Explain.

D. **The Lighting Circuits.**

18. With respect to resistance, why does parallel connection of lamps cause them to burn " bright " ?

19. With respect to resistance, why does series connection cause the lamps to burn " dim " ?

20. What is the reason for operating the tail light and the instrument board light in series?

E. **Fuses.**

21. Why are fuses used in electrical circuits? Locate the fuses in one make of automobile.

62. AUTOMOBILE ELECTRIC GENERATORS

The Generator, the Cut-out and Current Regulation

MATERIALS. Laboratory automobile with electric starting and lighting system; reference books.

NOTE. Review Experiment 18—The Electric Generator.

When a storage battery is used for ignition, starting and lighting an electric generator supplies current for charging the storage battery. See Experiment 22. The generator is usually operated from the crankshaft either by gear or chain drive or from the pump shaft. Since the engine runs at variable speeds the generator and the charging circuit must be so designed that, at medium speeds, the generator supplies a proper amount of current for the battery. At low speed the generator circuit must be entirely broken and at high speeds the current must not be excessive. This requires an automatic cut-out to break the circuit when the engine is idle or running slowly and a special type of winding in the generator coils or other regulating device to prevent too great a current at high speeds. Read *Motor Vehicles* and *The Gasoline Automobile.*

1. How does a single-unit starting and lighting system differ from a two-unit system?

2. Make a simple diagram of a lighting system without cut-out. See *Motor Vehicles*. Write in full the names of each part of the system.

3. Make a simple diagram of a starting and lighting system including the cut-out. See *Motor Vehicles*. Name all parts.

A. **The Automatic Cut-out.**

4. State the function of a cut-out in a charging circuit.

5. Which of the two coils of the cut-out causes the contact

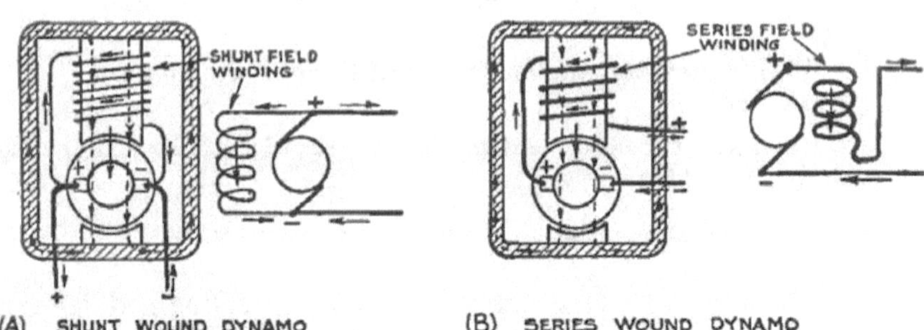

(A) SHUNT WOUND DYNAMO

(B) SERIES WOUND DYNAMO

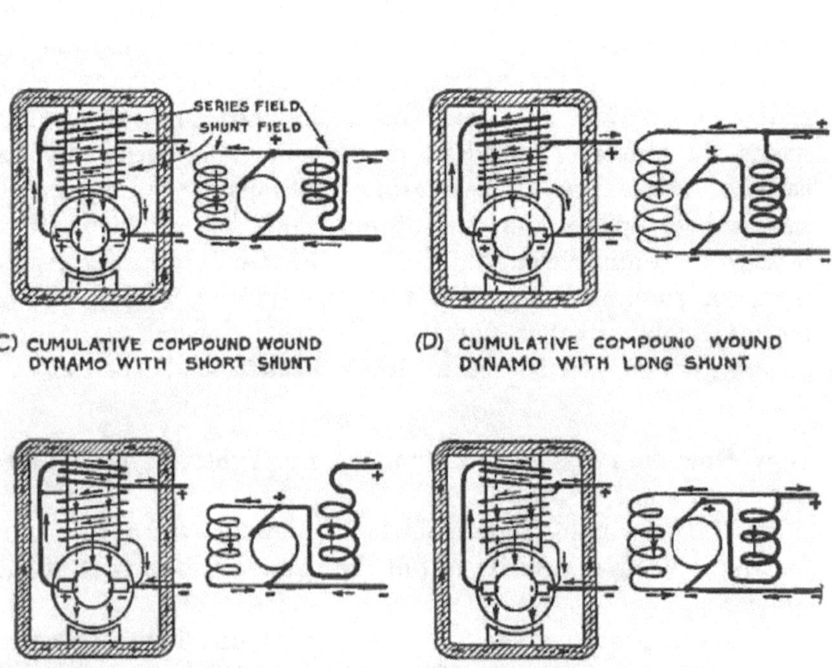

(C) CUMULATIVE COMPOUND WOUND DYNAMO WITH SHORT SHUNT

(D) CUMULATIVE COMPOUND WOUND DYNAMO WITH LONG SHUNT

(E) DIFFERENTIAL COMPOUND WOUND DYNAMO WITH SHORT SHUNT

(F) DIFFERENTIAL COMPOUND WOUND DYNAMO WITH LONG SHUNT

Fig. 75.—Types of dynamo field windings.

points to close? What causes the contact points to open when the magnetism in the core disappears?

6. To what are the wires of the coil which closes the cut-out attached? When does it close the cut-out?

7. The second coil on the cut-out core is part of what circuit?

8 How is this coil wound with respect to the winding of the coil referred to in question 5?

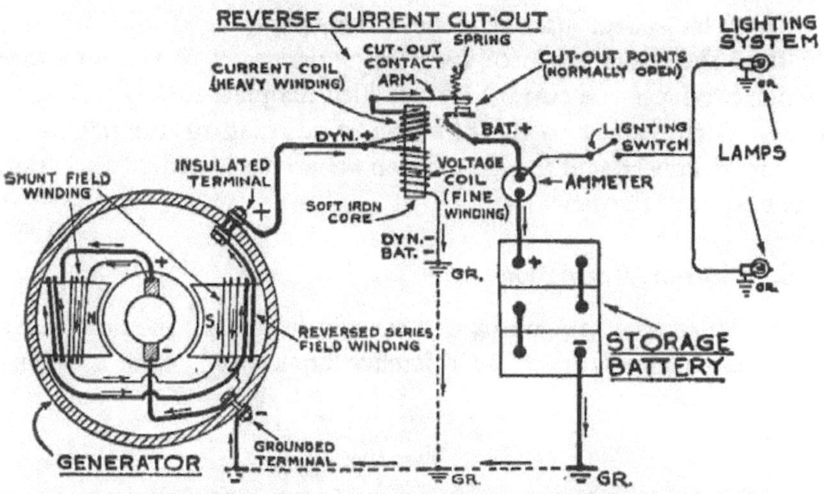

FIG. 76.—Wiring diagram of a generator, cut-out and storage battery. The generated current is regulated by reverse direction series field winding. Note also the reverse current cut-out.

9. Does the magnetism of the one coil increase or oppose the magnetism of the other?

10. How does the magnetism of one of the coils aid in causing the contact points to break? Explain the conditions which cause the contact points to break.

11. If a cut-out does not open when it should, what trouble may result?

B. **Third Brush Regulation of Generator Current.** Read this discussion in *The Gasoline Automobile.*

12. What type of armature winding is commonly used for this method of regulation?

13. Under what condition of speed are the lines of magnetic force through an armature coil fairly evenly distributed?

14. Under what condition of speed are the lines of force through the armature distorted?

15. To what regions of the field poles does this distortion shift the lines of force?

16. What effect upon the field magnetism is caused by this shift of the magnetic force away from that part of the armature which produces the current for the field magnetism?

17. With respect to the direction of rotation of the generator armature how should the third brush be moved in order to increase the output of the generator?

C. **Current Regulation.**

18. Study the method of current regulation on the laboratory automobile generator. Use reference books and write a report on it.

63. AUTOMOBILE STARTING MOTORS

The Motor, Starter Drives, and Troubles

MATERIALS. Laboratory automobile with electric starting and lighting system; reference books.

Automobile starting motors belonging to the two-unit systems are similar in construction to other direct-current motors. They are made with very heavy wires and heavy brushes for carrying large amperages at low voltage for the short period required to turn the engine over in starting. For reference use *The Gasoline Automobile.*

A. **The Starting Motor.**

1. What is the usual voltage for operating a starting motor?

2. About what amperage with the usual voltage is required to turn an automobile engine over?

3. How many watts and what horsepower does this represent? (Volts×amperes = watts) (746 watts = 1 horsepower).

4. What trouble may result from too frequent and prolonged use of the starting motor?

5. Why is a series-wound motor more satisfactory for this purpose than a shunt-wound motor? What is meant by starting torque of a motor?

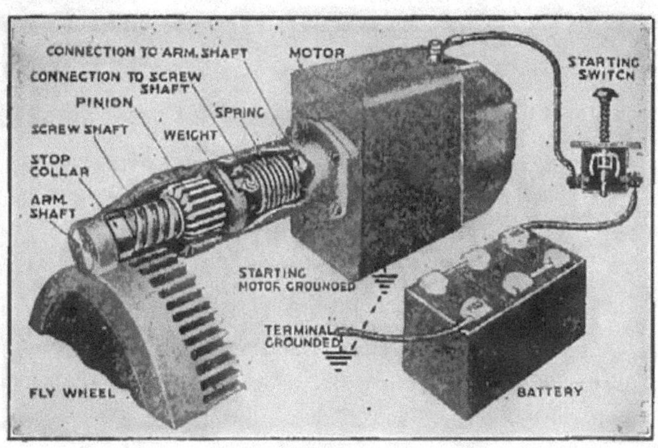

Fig. 77.—Typical Bendix drive starting motor.

6. Examine the starting motor on the laboratory automobile. State the number of (*a*) field poles, (*b*) brushes, (*c*) commutator segments.

7. Give the principal characteristics of the North East one-unit starter-generator.

8. Give the principal characteristics of the Delco one-unit starter-generator.

B. **Starter Drives.**

9. Name three types of drives.
10. Describe (*a*) the Bendix drive, (*b*) the magnetic drive.
11. What is the usual gear reduction in starter drive mechanisms?

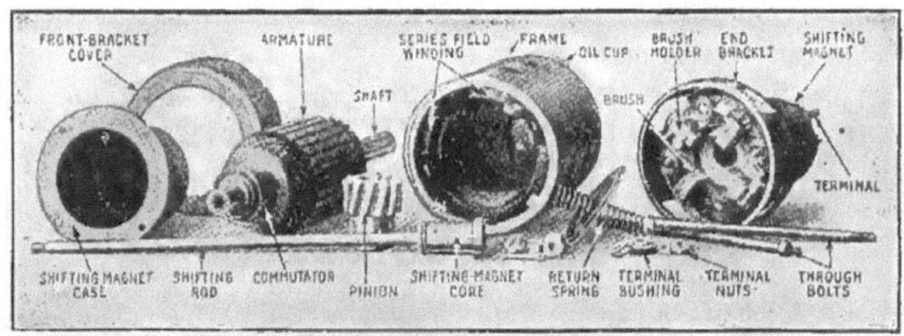

Fig. 78.—Parts of Westinghouse starting motor with electromagnetic pinion shift.

Fig. 79.—Westinghouse starting motor with automatic electromagnetic pinion shift.

C. **Starting Troubles.** See *The Gasoline Automobile.*

12. State possible troubles (*a*) at the battery terminals, (*b*) in the starting circuit wires, (*c*) at the brushes, (*d*) at the switch, (*e*) at the drive mechanism.

64. IGNITION TROUBLES AND ADJUSTMENTS

Spark Plugs, Wires, Timer, Induction Coil, Distributor, Battery, and Magneto

MATERIALS. Automobile engine; tools; reference books.

Remove the wires from the spark plugs of the engine. With an end wrench remove the spark plugs and examine them.

A. **Spark Plugs.**

1. Is there any deposit on the spark-plug porcelain and points? Name two sources from which this deposit may come.
2. How should spark plugs be cleaned?
3. Adjust the spark gap. How far apart should the points be?
4. How does the distance between the terminals of the points affect the spark?

Attach the wires to the plugs and lay them on the tops of the cylinders in such position that you can see the spark points as the engine is cranked. Turn on the ignition switch and observe the sparks.

5. In what sequence do the plugs fire? Consider the plug nearest the radiator as No. 1. In what sequence do the inlet valves open?
6. Does failure of a spark plug to fire when tested necessarily imply that the spark plug is at fault? Explain.
7. If one of four engine spark plugs is not firing, how could you find out which one it is? Give three methods.

B. **Wires.**

8. If the wires leading to the plugs were not connected to the proper plugs, how would you proceed to check up the wiring?
9. What is meant by a short-circuited primary wire? a short-circuited secondary wire?

10. Could an engine run (*a*) if the wire leading to one of the plugs were disconnected? (*b*) if one of the wires of the primary circuit were broken?

C. **The Timer.**

11. What trouble would probably result if the timer became dirty or if the breaker points were improperly adjusted?

12. What are the symptoms of improper adjustment of the spark advance mechanism?

D. **The Induction Coil.**

13. If the secondary wires of an induction coil were short-circuited, what would probably be the effect upon the operation of the spark plug?

14. What possible troubles may occur in the use of vibrating induction coils?

15. How might a condenser cause trouble?

E. **The Distributor.**

16. If the distributor became dirty or cracked, what trouble might result?

F. **The Battery.**

17. If battery terminals became corroded, what might be the result?

18. State one other common battery trouble.

G. **The Magneto.**

19. What trouble at the spark plugs might result from weak magnets in a magneto?

20. What would be the probable effect of excessive moisture upon a magneto?

21. What trouble in a magneto might be caused by dirt or excess of oil?

65. ENGINE MECHANICAL PARTS AND BEARINGS

The Crankshaft, the Camshaft, and the Connecting Rods

MATERIALS. **Laboratory engines and reference books.**

To avoid excessive wear and unnecessary noise it is very important that all bearings should be kept properly adjusted and lubricated. If bearings become loose, the friction surfaces wear away more rapidly, resulting in the weakening of essential mechanical parts, disagreeable engine knocks, and expensive repairs.

For reference work use Dyke.

A. The Crankshaft and the Main Bearings.

1. State the function of the crankshaft in an automobile.
2. What is the usual number of main bearings supporting the crankshaft in (*a*) a four-cylinder engine, (*b*) a six-cylinder engine?
3. To what parts of the engine are the main bearings attached?
4. What trouble would result if only the end bearings were used for supporting the crankshaft?
5. Why are bushings used in bearings? Of what materials are they made?
6. State the function of (*a*) the cap of a crankshaft or connecting-rod bearing, (*b*) shims. See Fig. 80.
7. Name two systems of lubrication by which oil may be supplied to the main bearings.
8. If a bearing becomes worn and loose what first adjustment may be necessary? What part may need renewal after further wear?
9. What is a counterbalanced crankshaft and what are its advantages?

B. **Connecting Rod and Bearings.**

10. Describe the construction of the bearing which fastens the connecting rod to the crankshaft.

11. Describe the construction of the wrist-pin bearing.

12. How does the Ford wrist-pin bearing differ from that of most other cars?

13. State two methods of lubricating wrist pins and crank pins.

C. **The Camshaft.**

14. In comparison with the speed of the crankshaft at what speed does the camshaft revolve and how is it operated?

15. Name the parts of a camshaft which involve friction and which are subject to wear.

16. A cam is a device for changing a rotary motion into what kind of motion?

17. Why does a cam which operates an exhaust valve usually have a broader nose than one which operates an intake valve?

18. What part of the valve mechanism does the cam push against?

19. In an old engine when cams become badly worn what effect is produced upon the valve operation?

20. What part of the lubrication system in some engines is operated by the camshaft?

21. Explain how the time gears and the camshaft are lubricated in one make of engine.

66. ENGINE KNOCKS

Knocks—Their Causes, Location, and Remedies

There are probably no more puzzling disorders for the average automobile owner than the varied types of engine knocks. In fact, with some of the more difficult knocks it frequently happens that a group of experienced repairmen will disagree among themselves as to the cause of the trouble. It is a time-consuming and an expensive procedure to begin by dismantling an engine before making a systematic diagnosis in order to determine the location and cause of a specific knock. A knock is usually a signal that some correction or adjustment is needed and it should not be ignored. Before looking for any mechanical trouble other possible causes of knocking should be carefully checked, such as (*a*) pre-ignition, (*b*) spark too far advanced, (*c*) defective carburetion, (*d*) incorrect valve clearance.

For reference use Dyke.

A. **Explosion Knocks Caused by Firing Out of Time.**

1. Explain how a knock is produced when a car goes up a steep hill with the spark too far advanced.

2. What is meant by pre-ignition? Why does pre-ignition cause a knock?

3. How might operating with a mixture that is too rich cause pre-ignition?

4. How could too much oil cause pre-ignition? How might an overheated engine cause pre-ignition?

5. Do pre-ignition knocks occur at all times? When do they occur?

6. How might the kind of lean mixture which causes an explosion in the carburetor also cause a slight knock?

7. How might an exhaust valve which does not close properly cause a slight knock?

B. **Knocks Caused by Loose Bearings and by Parts that Need Adjustment.** On account of wear in old engines loud knocks are common on crank main bearings, crank-pin bearings, and wrist-pin bearings. Occasionally in new engines knocks develop due to lack of proper adjustment of bearings or parts.

8. What causes piston slap?

9. State a test for loose pistons.

10. How is an iron or steel rod sometimes used for locating knocks ?

11. How does a connecting-rod bearing knock usually sound?

12. What is the best direct test for a loose wrist-pin bearing or a loose crank-pin bearing?

13. What adjustment can usually be made on lower connecting-rod bearings?

14. A knock which sounds like a double pound in very rapid succession should be located where?

15. How does a knock caused by pre-ignition or by having the spark too far advanced sound as compared with a crankshaft or a connecting-rod knock?

16. If a clicking noise occurs, where would you expect to locate it? What is usually the cause?

17. State a simple test for noisy valves.

18. How are noisy valves usually remedied?

Other occasional causes of knocks and noises are: a loose fly-wheel, loose cylinder nuts, poorly adjusted camshaft and time gears, or more remote parts of the car that may be loose and free to vibrate.

67. PISTONS AND CYLINDERS

MATERIALS. Automobile engine block; box containing pistons; rings; materials for manipulation.

In an automobile engine the pistons receive the expanding force of the explosion in the combustion chamber, and by means of the piston the energy of the exploding gases is transmitted to the connecting rod and to the crankshaft for driving the car. Examine a piston and connecting rod which have been removed from one of the laboratory engines. (The Ford.)

A. **Pistons.** For reference work, use Dyke; see **Engine Parts.**

1. Diagram (*a*) a piston in section, (*b*) a connecting rod, (*c*) a lap-joint piston ring, (*d*) a butt-joint piston ring.

2. What reasons can you give for making a gas-engine piston hollow?

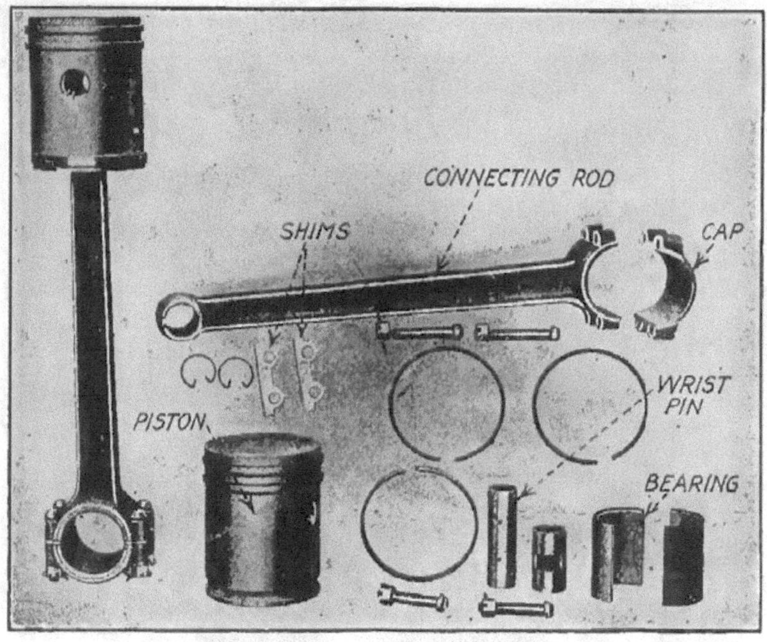

FIG. 80.—Piston, connecting rod and parts.

3. Is the force of the explosion exerted against the open end or the closed end?

4. What is the purpose of piston clearance?

5. Explain the function of the piston rings? How many rings are commonly used on each piston?

6. What is the function of an oil groove on the piston?

7. In the more common types of automobile engines how do the pistons receive their oil?

8. How are new piston rings put on a piston?

9. Mention five causes of compression leakage due to defects in piston rings. See Dyke—index.

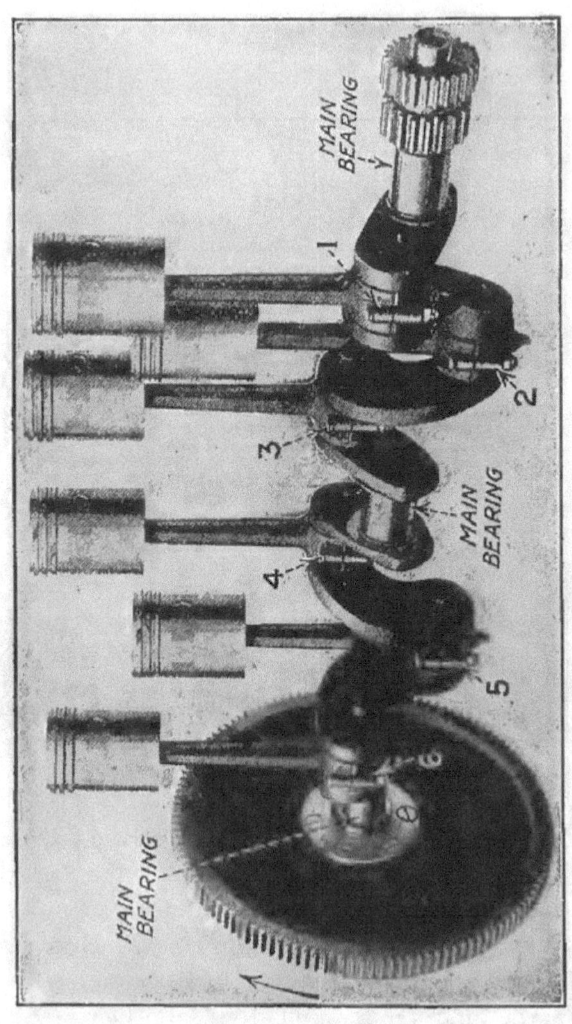

Fig. 81.—Six-cylinder crankshaft with three main bearings, connecting rods and pistons.

10. What is the function of the wrist pin and of what metal is it commonly made?

B. **Manipulation.** Read Dyke on the removal of piston rings.

(*a*) With the necessary tools as described in Dyke remove all of the piston rings from one of the pistons. Special care should be taken to avoid spreading the rings more than is necessary to insert the thin metal strips. Carelessness in this respect may result in either breaking the rings or bending them so that they fail to fit properly. If you are in doubt as to the procedure inquire of the instructor. When all rings are removed from one piston have the work approved by the instructor.

(*b*) Read Dyke on "Fitting Rings to Pistons." Replace the rings on the piston and show the piston to the instructor.

(*c*) Fit a piston, with rings attached, into an engine cylinder. Have this job inspected, then remove the piston and place it in the supply box as found at the beginning.

C. **Cylinders.** For reference read Dyke.

11. State the characteristics of a well-made cylinder.

12. State the advantages and disadvantages of T-head and L-head engines.

13. Describe two types of cylinder construction other than the T head and the L head.

14. What is meant by (*a*) stroke, (*b*) bore, (*c*) piston displacement?

15. State the stroke and the bore of five well-known makes of cars. See Dyke, "Specifications of Leading Cars."

68. ENGINE POWER

Calculating the Power of a Gas Engine

When a pound weight is lifted vertically through a distance of 1 foot, 1 foot-pound of work is done. The foot-pound is the unit of work. When 50 pounds are lifted through a distance of 1 foot,

50 foot-pounds of work are done. If 50 pounds are lifted through 10 feet, the work done is 500 foot-pounds. To find the foot-pounds of work done in any mechanical operation multiply push or pull in pounds by the distance in feet through which the thing pushed or pulled is moved.

The power of an engine depends upon how much work it can do per minute (per unit of time). If an engine is able to lift 33,000 pounds through a distance of 1 foot in one minute, that engine is considered able to do work at the rate of 1 horsepower. The same engine may lift 1 pound through a distance of 33,000 feet, etc. In general, if an engine does 33,000 foot-pounds of work in a minute it is said to work at the rate of a horsepower. An engine that does 66,000 foot-pounds of work in a minute is a 2-horsepower engine, etc.

To find the horsepower of an engine find how many foot-pounds of work it does per minute and divide this result by 33,000.

1. In going up a hill an automobile engine lifts a 3,000-pound car through a vertical difference of level (vertical height of the hill, not the slope) of 200 feet in one minute. Find how much work is done and what horsepower is required to do this work in this time. Disregard all friction.

2. Does friction increase or decrease the power required to do an actual piece of work such as that in problem 1. Mention three sources of friction in this situation.

3. With a foot rule measure the diameter of the cylinder of the laboratory four-stroke engine. Measure also the length of stroke in nches (distance between the extreme outward and the extreme inward position of the piston). Have these measurements approved by the instructor before proceeding further. Calculate the area of the face of the piston in square inches. Use two decimal places only.

4. Assuming that the average pressure during the power stroke is 90 pounds per square inch, calculate the average pressure on the total face of the piston during the power stroke.

5. Ask the instructor for a speed indicator. Place it against the engine crankshaft and determine the number of revolutions per minute. (Run the engine at maximum speed.)

6. Calculate the work done in one power stroke. (Total pressure in pounds on the piston times length of stroke in feet.)

7. In a four-stroke engine note that every fourth stroke is a power stroke. How much work can this engine do per minute when it is running at the rate of 500 revolutions per minute? (Refer to question 6.)

8. Based on the above calculations, what horsepower has this engine? (Work per minute divided by 33,000.) Assume that on account of friction the engine delivers 75 per cent of the indicated power.

9. What is the S. A. E. formula for calculating the horsepower of a gas engine? See *Motor Vehicles*.

10. Calculate the horsepower of the engine used above by the S. A. E. formula. This formula is based upon a piston speed of 1,000 feet per minute. How far does this piston move per revolution (out and back)? How far in feet does it move per minute? If the piston speed of this engine is less than 1,000 feet per minute the power will be in porportion to the piston speed.

11. Calculate the horsepower of the Ford engine by the S. A. E. formula.

69. STEERING GEAR, MUFFLER, WHEELS, AND BEARINGS

MATERIALS. Laboratory automobiles and reference books.

A. **Steering Gears.** Read *The Gasoline Automobile* and *Motor Vehicles*.

1. Why is the front axle of an automobile rigid as compared with that of a horse-drawn vehicle?

2. Describe the location of the following parts of the steering-gear mechanism: (*a*) steering knuckle, (*b*) tie rod, (*c*) drag link, (*d*) steering-lever arm, (*e*) steering-knuckle arm. See Fig. 31.

3. Distinguish between reversible and irreversible steering gears.

4. What kind of steering gear has the Ford car—reversible or irreversible?

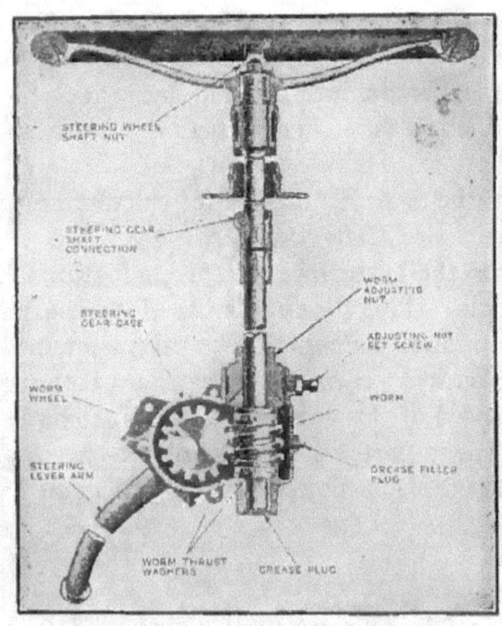

FIG. 82.—Worm and wheel steering gear.

5. Name one other make of car with which you are familiar and state whether the steering gear is reversible or irreversible.

6. Explain how camber makes the steering mechanism work more easily.

7. How does a worm and wheel type of gear mechanism used in some cars provide for adjusting in case of wear?

B. **Mufflers.**

8. Diagram two commercial types of muffler design.

9. Approximately what is the pressure of the expanding gas in the cylinder when the exhaust valve opens?

10. How does a muffler affect engine power?

11. What are the characteristics of an efficient muffler?

12. What is the function of a cut-out placed on the exhaust pipe?

C. **Wheels.**

13. State three kinds of strains that automobile wheels must withstand.

14. Under what conditions of strain are wooden wheels most likely to break?

15. What kind of wood is used for making wooden wheels?

16. Why are wheels dished?

17. What advantages over wooden wheels are claimed for wire wheels?

18. What claims are offered in favor of pressed steel wheels?

D. **Bearings.**

19. State three kinds of bearings in common use on automobiles.

20. What kind of bearings are commonly used for crankshaft main bearings? Why?

21. Name three important parts of an automobile which usually operate on roller bearings.

70. CHASSIS ARRANGEMENT, FRAMES, AND SPRINGS

MATERIALS. Laboratory automobiles and reference books.

Read *The Gasoline Automobile* and *Motor Vehicles.*

A. Chassis Arrangement.

1. What is the advantage of a three-point suspension for the power plant instead of four points?
2. What is meant by the expression unit power plant?
3. Name three possible positions for the change gears.
4. What objection may be made to placing the change gears on the rear axle?

B. Frames.

5. Of what kind of steel are frames made?
6. Why are frames usually riveted together?
7. What is the function of the reinforcing plates?
8. Why is the frame usually made deeper at the center than at the ends?
9. Why is the frame made narrow at the front?
10. Describe the Ford frame.
11. Describe the power-plant suspension on the Ford.
12. Describe the power-plant suspension on one other make of automobile.
13. What is a sub-frame? Name one make of car which uses this construction.

C. Springs.

14. What is a laminated leaf spring?
15. State the function of the following parts: (*a*) the center bolt, (*b*) the spring clip, (*c*) the eyes, (*d*) the spring blocks, (*e*) the master leaf.

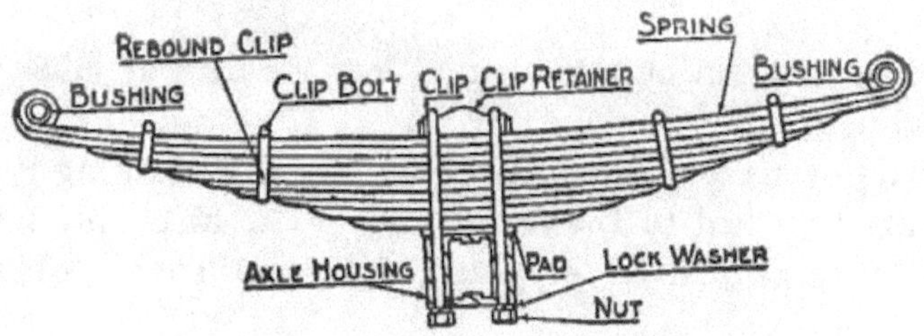

Fig. 83.—Laminated leaf spring.

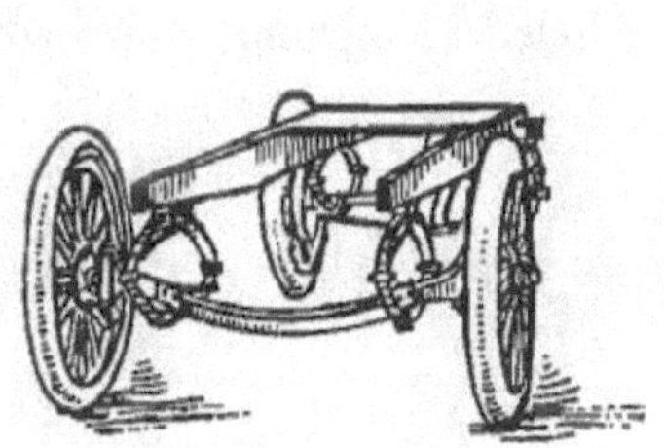

Fig. 84.—Full elliptic spring.

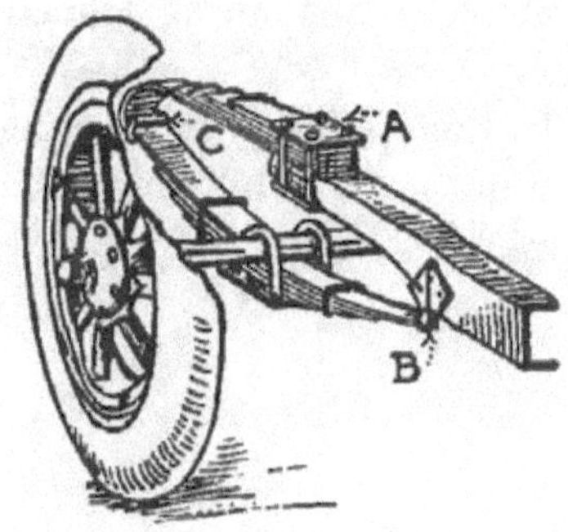

Fig. 85.—Three-quarters elliptic spring.

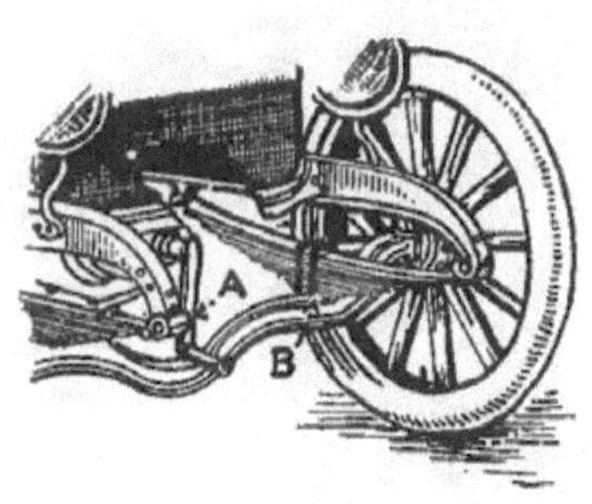

Fig. 86.—Semi-elliptic spring.

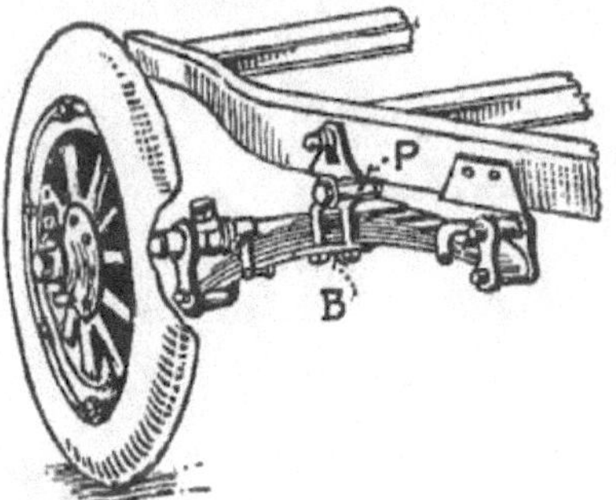

Fig. 87.—Cantilever spring.

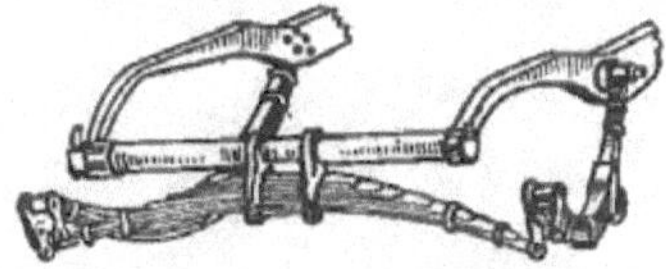

Fig. 88.—Platform Springs.

16. Make a diagram of a laminated leaf spring and label the parts named in question 15.

17. Explain or make diagrams showing how the following types of springs are attached to the frame and to the axle: (*a*) semi-elliptical, (*b*) three-quarter elliptical, (*c*) cantilever, (*d*) full elliptical.

18. Describe the spring suspension of the Ford car.

19. Describe the spring suspension of one other make of automobile.

20. In the operation of a spring, where does friction occur?

21. What kind of lubricant should be used on springs and how is it applied?

REFERENCE BOOKS

A. Laboratory Reference Shelf—Required Books.

The Gasoline Automobile—Hobbs, Elliott, and Consoliver McGraw-Hill Book Co., Inc., N. Y.	3 copies
Motor Vehicles and Their Engines—Frazer and Jones . D. Van Nostrand Co., N. Y.	3 copies
Automobile and Gasoline Engine Encyclopedia—Dyke A. L. Dyke, St. Louis, Mo.	3 copies
The Ford Manual . . . . The Ford Motor Co., Detroit, Mich.	3 copies
The Model T Ford Car—Pagé . . Norman W. Henley Publishing Co., N. Y.	3 copies
Practical Physics—Black and Davis The Macmillan Co., N. Y.	2 copies
Practical Physics—Millikan, Gale, and Pyle . . . . . . Ginn & Co., N. Y.	2 copies
Gasoline Automobiles—Moyer . . . . McGraw-Hill Book Co., Inc., N. Y.	2 copies

B. Reference Books and Related Books.

Automobile Questions and Answers—Pagé.
Norman W. Henley Publishing Co., N. Y.

Automotive Repair—Wright
John Wiley & Sons, N. Y.

Modern Starting, Lighting and Ignition Systems—Pagé.
Norman W. Henley Publishing Co., N. Y.

Gas Engine Ignition—Norris, Winning and Weaver.
McGraw-Hill Book Co., Inc., N. Y.

Farm Motors—Potter.
McGraw-Hill Book Co., Inc., N. Y.

Gasoline and Kerosene Carburetors—Pagé.
Norman W. Henley Publishing Co., N. Y.

The Modern Gasoline Automobile—Pagé.
Norman W. Henley Publishing Co., N. Y.
Storage Batteries Simplified—Pagé.
Norman W. Henley Publishing Co., N. Y.
Aviation Engines—Pagé.
Norman W. Henley Publishing Co., N. Y.
Motor-cycles Side Cars and Cycle Cars—Pagé.
Norman W. Henley Publishing Co., N. Y.
Automobile Charts—Pagé.
Location of Gasoline Engine Troubles.
Location of Carburetion Troubles.
Location of Ignition System Troubles.
Location of Cooling and Lubricating Troubles.
Location of Starting and Lighting System Faults.
Location of Ford Engine Troubles.
Location of Motor Cycle Troubles.
Lubrication of the Motor Car Chassis.
Norman W. Henley Publishing Co., N. Y.

APPARATUS LIST

NOTE. The letters S. S. in this list refer to the Standard Scientific Co. New York.

EXPERIMENTS

1. Automobile Mechanisms—A.

1–*a*. One of the typical automobiles either new or used. Mount both front and rear axles on a strong wooden stand so that wheels are clear of the ground.

4. The Gasoline Engine—A.

4–*a*. Gasoline engine. Sears, Roebuck & Co., Chicago, Ill.
4–*b*. Ignition-bottle. Heavy glass, narrow bottle, height 10 inches, diameter 1½ inches. S. S. Or use narrow olive bottle.
4–*c*. Rubber tube. S. S.
4–*d*. Dry cells. Any electrical supply house.
4–*e*. Telephone magneto with small lamp. S. S.

6. Carburetors—A.

6–*a*. Bunsen burner, Terrill's. S. S.
6–*b*. Ignition-bottle. Same as in 4-*b*.
6–*c*. Large glass jar or pail.
6–*d*. Sectional carburetor. Use Sectional Holley Model G, Holley Bros. Co., Detroit, Mich., or other simple type of carburetor.

7. Carburetors—B.

7–*a*. Purchase simple carburetors from used-car dealers. Schebler Model E and Kingston Model E. For addresses of manufacturers see Dyke.

8. **Automobile Engine—A.**

8–*a*. Ford chassis. New or used chassis. Remove the radiator, the cylinder head, the dashboard, the transmission cover, the bottom plate, and one piston with connecting rod. Mount both front and rear axles on a wooden stand so that wheels are clear of the ground. For electrical work mount the induction-coil box on the frame at the left side of the engine. A separate wooden stand should be provided for supporting the rear spring so that the rear axle may be completely taken off.

13. **Introductory Electrical Work—A.**

13–*a*. Base block 5×5×2 inches. S. S.
13–*b*. Round battery jar $5\frac{1}{2}$ inches high by $2\frac{3}{4}$ inches diameter. S. S.
13–*c*. Ammonium chloride (sal ammoniac) technical. S. S.
13–*d*. Zinc battery rod. S. S.
13–*e*. Carbon rod from an old dry cell.
13–*f*. Bunsen burner, Terrill's. S. S.
13–*g*. Electric bell. Any electrical supply house, or S. S.
13–*h*. No. 24 insulated wire, double cotton. S. S.
13–*i*. Nitric acid. S. S.

14. **Introductory Electrical Work—B.**

14–*a*. Battery voltmeter, mounted. S. S.
14–*b*. 35-ampere battery ammeter, mounted. S. S.
14–*c*. Push-button. S. S.

15. **Introductory Electrical Work—C.**

15–*a*. Ring stand. S. S.
15–*b*. Ring-stand clamps. S. S.
15–*c*. 3-volt lamps. S. S.
15–*d*. Small 3-volt motor. S. S.
15–*e*. Electric bell. S. S.
15–*f*. Battery voltmeter. S. S.
15–*g*. 35-ampere battery ammeter, mounted. S. S.
15–*h*. Push-button. S. S.

16. **Introductory Electrical Work—D.**

16–*a*. Compass, pocket. S. S.
16–*b*. Push-button. S. S.
16–*c*. Electric bell. S. S.

17. The Electric Motor.

17–a. St. Louis motor. S. S.
17–b. 35-ampere battery ammeter, mounted. S. S.

18. The Electric Generator.

18–a. Small hand-power generator. L. E. Knott Apparatus Co., Boston, Mass. No. 97–148.
18–b. Small lamp. S. S.
18–c. 35-ampere battery ammeter. S. S.
18–d. Battery voltmeter. S. S.
18–e. Electric bell. S. S.
18–f. Small 3-volt motor. S. S.
18–g. Telephone magneto-generator. S. S.

19. Ignition Systems—A.

19–a. Vibrating induction coil. Sears, Roebuck & Co., Chicago. No. 6A9234, or S. S.
19–b. Metal-ring stand. S. S.
19–c. Automobile spark plug. Any automobile supply house.

20. Ignition Systems—B.

20–a. Use same coil listed in experiment 19.
20–b. Metal-ring stands. S. S.
20–c. Wooden block with four binding posts to represent a distributor. S. S.
20–d. Non-vibrating induction coil (make-and-break spark coil). Sears, Roebuck & Co., Chicago.

21. Storage Battery—A.

21–a. Simple demonstration battery with sheet lead plates. S. S.
21–b. Battery voltmeter, mounted. S. S.
21–c. Electric bell. Any electrical store or S. S.
21–d. 2-volt lamp. S. S.
21–e. Small 2-volt motor. S. S.
21–f. Lamp board and 1-ampere lamp. S. S.

29. Valve Mechanisms—A.

29–a. Valve-spring compressor. Automobile supply house.

30. Valve Mechanisms—B.

30–*a*. Valve push-rod with adjustment screw. Dealer in automobile junk.

30–*b*. Valve grinding tools. Automobile supply house.

31. Ignition Induction Coils.

31–*a*. Vibrating induction coil. Sears, Roebuck & Co., Chicago No. 6A9234, or S. S.

31–*b*. Make-and-break coil. Sears, Roebuck & Co.

31–*c*. Automobile induction coil. Dealer in used automobile supplies.

32. Ignition Systems—C.

32–*a*. Atwater-Kent ignition unit; type CC. Dealer in used ignition systems or Atwater-Kent Co., Philadelphia, Pa.

32–*b*. Spark plugs. Any dealer.

32–*c*. Ring stands. S. S.

34. Ignition Systems—E.

33–*a*. Remy Model RL ignition system. Dealer in used ignition parts or Remy Electric Co., Anderson, Ind.

35. Ignition Systems—F.

35–*a*. Dealer in used parts or manufacturers, Bosch, type DV4 high-tension magneto. Bosch Magneto Co., N. Y. Or Eisemann type G4 high-tension magneto, Eisemann Magneto Co., N. Y. Or Dixie magneto, Splitdorf Co., Newark, N. J.

36. Storage Battery—B.

36–*a*. Small lead storage battery in glass jar. Central Scientific Co., Chicago. No. 1042 No. B. Write for catalogs to Electric Storage Battery Co., Philadelphia, Pa., and Willard Storage Battery Co., Cleveland, O.

36–*b*. Battery hydrometer. Automobile supply dealer or Willard Storage Battery Co., Cleveland, O.

36–*c*. Buy lamp sockets from any electrical dealer and make up a lamp board resistance or buy a suitable rheostat from S. S.

47. Tires—A.

47–*a*. Tire levers. Automobile dealer.
47–*b*. Tire pump. Dealer.

48. Tires—B.

48–*a*. Tube bag. Dealer.
48–*b*. Cement and patches. Dealer.
48–*c*. Five-minute vulcanizer. Dealer.

50. Carburetors—C.

50–*a*. Carburetors. Dealer in used parts or an automobile junk dealer or write to the manufacturers. For addresses see Dyke.

51. Carburetors—D.

51–*a*. Schebler Model E. Dealer in used parts or Wheeler & Schebler, Indianapolis, Ind.
51–*b*. Kingston Model E. Dealer in used parts or Byrne, Kingston & Co., Kokomo, Ind.
51–*c*. Holley Model G. Dealer in used parts or from Holley Bros. Co., Detroit, Mich.

54. Fuel Feed Systems.

54–*a*. Stewart vacuum tank. Purchase a sectional tank from the manufacturers, Stewart Warner Speedometer Corp., Chicago, Ill., or buy a vacuum tank from a dealer in used parts.

57. Differential—A.

57–*a*. Small Meccano model of a differential. Meccano Co., Inc., N. Y.

59. Alternating Currents.

59–*a*. Pocket compass. S. S.
59–*b*. Telephone magneto. S. S.
59–*c*. Battery voltmeter. S. S.
59–*d*. Electric bell. S. S.
59–*e*. Large coils of 1000 turns. S. S.

61. Automobile Electric Circuits—C.

61–*a*. Electric generator (etc.). Use apparatus for experiment 18.

61–*b*. Telegraph sounder. S. S.

61–*c*. Automobile cut-out. Dealer in automobile ignition parts.

67. Pistons and Cyliders.

67–*a*. Use a Ford piston and the Ford engine cylinder.

INDEX

Zeitfracht Medien GmbH
Ferdinand-Jühlke-Straße 7
99095 Erfurt, Deutschland
produktsicherheit@kolibri360.de